To Joan
Tom B___

Deborah White

Marc Evans

Rare Wildflowers *of* Kentucky

Thomas G. Barnes, Deborah White & Marc Evans

THE UNIVERSITY PRESS OF KENTUCKY

Editorial and Sales Offices: The University Press of Kentucky
663 South Limestone Street, Lexington, Kentucky 40508–4008
www.kentuckypress.com

12 11 10 09 08   5 4 3 2 1

Library of Congress Cataloging-in-Publication Data
Barnes, Thomas G., 1957–
Rare wildflowers of Kentucky / Thomas G. Barnes,
Deborah L. White, and Marc Evans.
    p. cm.
Includes bibliographical references and index.
ISBN 978-0-8131-2496-4 (hardcover : alk. paper)
1. Wild flowers—Kentucky—Identification. 2. Rare plants—
Kentucky—Identification. 3. Wild flowers—Kentucky—
Pictorial works. 4. Rare plants—Kentucky—Pictorial works.
I. White, Deborah L. II. Evans, Marc, 1952– III. Title.
QK162.B36 2008
582.1309769—dc22

                    2007047704

Manufactured in China
Design and typesetting by Julie Allred, BW&A Books, Inc.

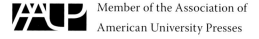 Member of the Association of
American University Presses

Contents

Kentucky, and our nation as a whole, is changing right before our eyes. As we travel across the commonwealth, we see how much of the landscape is altered, some temporarily, some permanently: housing and industrial development sites appear almost overnight; more timber is harvested, complete with logging roads, skid trails, and soil washing down slopes; another mountain is lost to the ravages of mountaintop coal removal.

Change is inevitable, but these changes have costs associated with them in the loss of precious natural resources. Native plants and animals need some place to call home, and we keep destroying their homes to make our own homes better or more comfortable or to make our own lives easier. No one wants to deny others the opportunities to make their lives better, but we often do not recognize the true costs that are associated with the lifestyle choices we make. These costs go far beyond the economic. This book addresses one of those costs: the loss of native plants.

The focus of this book, much like that of an earlier book, *Kentucky's Last Great Places,* is conservation. We hope to catch your eye with the striking, deep orange color of Indian paintbrush or the delicate texture of the Allegheny-vine or the un-usual shape of the southern monkshood flower. We hope that after viewing the plates, you will read the text to learn about how our lifestyle choices have affected the habitats of rare plants in Kentucky. In these pages you can find out why plants become rare, which species are rare in our state, and why we should protect rare plants and animals. Some scientists have estimated that we can protect more than 80 percent of the rare organisms if we just protect the ecological communities they reside in. This book contains brief community descriptions so that you can understand where these precious plants occur.

Although we present a great deal of technical information about rare plant conservation, we have placed most of that information at the back of the book so that it does not get in the way of a casual reading of the text or viewing of the images. You can obtain further information about the rare plants of Kentucky by visiting the Kentucky State Nature Preserves Commission (KSNPC) Web page and its rare plant database (www.naturepreserves.ky.gov), as well as Natureserve Explorer (www.natureserve.org/explorer), the sources for some of the information in this book.

Thomas G. Barnes

There were moments of both great joy and great sadness and disappointment in preparing this book. I was thrilled when I found a new plant species in the state, one not recorded before. It was a native toadflax, an annual and Coastal Plain species that my friends Susan Wilson and Chris and Mary Alice Bidwell found in Ballard County. There was also the thrill of discovering in Whitley County, in a power-line right-of-way, perhaps the largest population of nettle-leaf sage, several hundred plants, many in flower. There were those rare days when I photographed as many as five species on the 2004 Kentucky State Nature Preserves Rare, Threatened and Endangered List, and there were other days when I photographed no plants on the list. Of all the hikes, the most spectacular one was in mid-August, with stifling heat and humidity, a 2.6-mile trek straight up to White Rocks at Cumberland Gap National Historical Park. With a gain of 3,000 feet in elevation, carrying a camera backpack and tripod in that weather, I felt a sense of accomplishment just making it to the summit, and then elation at being able to photograph the two species I was after that day. Such a day was not merely good but fantastic.

Some days were not so fantastic. There was the day I was with Deborah White, one of my co-authors, on a trip to the Daniel Boone National Forest to find the ovate catchfly. We went to a site and located a handful of plants where there should have been dozens, and not one was in flower. Though that was bad enough, the rest of the day went sour quickly. We visited another site that had been heavily logged, where the plants we were looking for were gone, and the forest understory had developed into a thicket of small-flowered or white-flowered leafcup. The worst was yet to come. We went over a hill and found an entire wet meadow, more than 20 or 30 acres in full flower, of the invasive exotic purple loosestrife. Another time I was provided information on the location of the diminutive and early-flowering sweet pinesap. I located the plants from the directions given, but they were not in flower yet, and I planned a trip back in a week. On the return trip, I placed my camera on my tripod and headed down the trail because I had a limited amount of time to get the images and return home. As I approached the location, I was intensely focusing my attention on the plants rather than the path. Then a tree root sprang forth from the earth and grabbed my ankle—actually, I just tripped on the dang root and took a tumble, camera, tripod, and all, landing on a cut pitch pine stump. Immediate pain: I knew I had broken some ribs. I also knew there was nothing that could be done for broken ribs, and so I picked up the gear, checked to make sure it worked, and walked the remaining 100 yards to the plants. I spent an hour or more photographing them, attempting not to move much because of the pain. Then I walked out a half mile to my car and drove to the doctor's office.

In the end, though, I was grateful for the opportunity to travel across this beautiful state, get into some wonderful natural areas, make some great new friends, and photograph some of the most beautiful plants you can ever imagine. This turned into a spectacular adventure. Of the original 2004 list of 300 plants that I worked from, I missed only about 90 species, and most of these were mosses, sedges, rushes, and grasses. I missed those because it was almost impossible to get every single species in one growing season. I was able to photograph some of the more easily accessible species that will represent those groups. One of the limitations is that it is pretty difficult to make grasses, sedges, and rushes photogenic. The species that are in the book will, I hope, make you appreciate the various colors, forms, textures, and intricacies of plants that most Kentuckians will never see in their home state. I also hope it will spur you to take some action to slow or even stop the loss of plants, and other species, from this state and country.

When I began this project, I thought it would be relatively easy to complete the task of getting photographs of rare plants. After all, the Kentucky State Nature Preserves has a database with location information that they use to monitor these species. This assumption proved to be so far off the mark that at times I began to wonder about my abilities to find my way in the woods. Just because you have a dot on a map and maybe a description doesn't mean that the plant is still there or the habitat hasn't changed or the plants are in flower—or maybe I was just a biologist lost in the woods. This proved to be a challenge, and I remember one day, a good one, when Doug Stevens, a retired Kentucky Fish and Wildlife Fisheries biologist, and I went looking for nettle-leaf sage near Lake Cumberland. We followed the directions and found the general location, and then we looked and looked, fearing the plants were no longer in those rocky woods. After much searching, we found about half a dozen plants, but only two had flowered, and that had been more than two weeks before. This was a good day because we found the plants, but it was a sad day because those plants are doomed: trees close the canopy and the habitat changes from open woodland/rocky savanna to closed-canopy forest. Through this process of researching, finding, and photographing rare plants, I have gained an enormous amount of respect for what KSNPC botanists do for a living. It is tough, challenging work.

Throughout the time I spent getting images for the book, I began to feel like a dinosaur of sorts, as the photographic world was rapidly converting from film to digital. I began this project using film and shot the entire book using film, although it will probably be the last film-based project I do. My film of choice was Fuji Velvia 50 or 100, and my camera equipment was the old standby Nikon F100. My lens of preference was the Nikkor 200 micro, but I used Nikkor lenses ranging from 17 mm to 500 mm while getting images for the book. For example, in the case of the Kentucky lady's-slipper orchids, I wanted to compress space and be very selective in my background and used the 500-mm lens for that image; I did the same for the image of Canada yew because that species grew on an inaccessible cliff line. Most of the images were taken with available light, although some were made with balanced fill flash. (I used a Nikon SB 26 flash, which provided that source of fill.) Finally, all images were made with the camera and lens sitting on top of a Gitzo carbon fiber tripod with an Arca Swiss ball head.

Thomas G. Barnes

Acknowledgments

TGB

First and foremost, I am greatly indebted to my co-authors, Deborah White and Marc Evans of the Kentucky State Nature Preserves Commission, for writing most of the text for this book. Their intimate knowledge and love of plants, ecology, and Kentucky shine through in their prose. They have become close colleagues and dear friends, and I appreciate all that they do on a daily basis in helping conserve the rich biological diversity of Kentucky. Without them, this book would not be a reality. I must acknowledge my two children, Jeremiah and Michaela, who often had to endure my taking them to places they may not have wanted to go just so I could photograph some silly plants, as they called them. They were troupers, and I love them dearly. To the people who helped me find plants—I am sure I will forget someone, so please accept my apologies up front if you are not mentioned—I am deeply indebted, but I also want you to know that I am so grateful for making many new friends in this process. These folks include Doug Stevens, Kim Feeman, Bryan Wender, Bob Dunlap, Dan Boone, Julian Campbell, Kyle Napier, Ben Begley, Bart Jones, Dennis Horn, Ed Chester, Ed Hartowitz, James Kiser, Dan Dourson, Eugene Wofford, and most especially Dewayne Estes. Thank you from the bottom of my heart for your help. Three other individuals, Chris and Mary Alice Bidwell and Susan Wilson, also deserve special thanks for their companionship and friendship on many photographic endeavors. As I have aged, and, I hope, become wiser, I realize I probably shouldn't be in remote locations without someone to help in case something goes wrong. What a group we made, two aging men, looking scruffy with ugly beards, and two lovely women, out in the fields and forests, carrying a bunch of camera gear around in search of unique plants. I have had such wonderful field experiences with these friends that they are like family to me, and I care deeply about them. The fact that they are nurses gave me some comfort—I knew that if I did something stupid, they had the medical expertise to help. I wish also to thank the chair of my department at the University of Kentucky, Dr. Steve Bullard, who supported me financially and professionally without reservation while I was working on this project. Finally, I wish to thank my parents, Ola and Donna Barnes, who have been a source of emotional support throughout my entire life.

ME

I would like to thank Tom for asking me to be part of this project. I am so lucky to have a job that allows me the opportunities to visit and explore the diverse natural areas of Kentucky. For that I thank the Nature Preserves Commission. It is through these experiences that I have gained a better understanding and greater appreciation of the many beautiful natural communities that grace our state.

DLW

I am honored that Tom Barnes asked me to contribute to this book to showcase the beauty of rare plants. Also, I am grateful to my fellow authors and friends, Tom and Marc, for their help, as well as to reviewers and editors, and to my family for their support. As a botanist at the Kentucky State Nature Preserves Commission, I have had the opportunity to learn about Kentucky's remarkable flora. It is great place to work and I am grateful to all the people who support it and other conservation programs.

Rare Wildflowers of Kentucky

Introduction

THE KENTUCKY LANDSCAPE is changing faster than ever. Local forests are replaced by housing developments, and the stores and gas stations that follow expand the edges of towns farther and farther into the countryside. Roads in the remotest part of the state often lead to houses tucked under the trees. Natural resources are needed for materials and energy to support the people who live and work here, and the harvest and use of these resources translates into changes to the land. A 2005 report by Natureserve and its partners states that runaway development could threaten one in three imperiled species. We have sprawled into habitat for prairie gentian, swamp candles, and yellow-crested orchid. This book explores the decline in natural areas and the associated decline in native Kentucky plants, particularly those in jeopardy of becoming extinct.

According to a report developed by the researchers Wilcove and Master in 2005 for Natureserve, 17 percent of vascular plants (basically excluding mosses and closely related plant groups)—8,272 plants nationwide—are at risk of extinction. The situation is similar in Kentucky. As of the beginning of 2007, 273 plant species in our state were considered endangered or threatened. An additional 57 were listed as of special concern, species that are evidently declining and have the potential to be added to the official list. Six plants are considered extirpated, or eliminated, from the state, and one of these, stipuled scurfpea, is globally extinct. Another indication that Kentucky is losing its native flora is that 60 plant species in this state have not been seen in 20 or more years and are considered "historic." Kentucky State Nature Preserves Commission (KSNPC), the agency mandated by the Kentucky legislature to monitor the native flora and identify plants that are endangered, has added 24 plants to this list of historic plants in the last five years, which may indicate that more plants are becoming rarer and more likely to be extirpated from the state.

One way to protect native plants is to purchase land where they occur. It is unlikely that the funding will be able to keep up with the decline in our native flora; it has not so far. About 20 percent of listed rare plants, 62, do not occur on any federal, state-owned, or private conservation lands. Of those plants that do occur on public or private conservation lands, 75 are represented by a single occurrence, and the majority

Canada anemone historically occurred in central Kentucky.

Ear-leaf false foxglove occurs on public land that is purchased specifically for the protection of biodiversity.

Rose pogonia orchid occurs in one location and is protected by a private landowner.

Soft-haired thermopsis can be found in the Daniel Boone National Forest; it is an example of a species that occurs on public land but is not managed specifically for the protection of biodiversity.

have fewer than four. One or a few protected occurrences of these plants are far short of what is needed to ensure that they can sustain themselves in the Kentucky landscape. National guidelines, which are based on natural heritage methods used in all 50 states to evaluate endangered species, suggest about 100 populations are needed to consider a plant species completely secure. Also, public lands are purchased for a variety of reasons, such as forestry, wildlife management, and military uses, and, though they may contribute to biodiversity protection, that is one consideration among many in the management of the land. About 113 rare plants have at least one occurrence on lands established and managed specifically for biodiversity protection and with legal safeguards against conversion to other public uses.

Obviously, private lands are important in determining the fate of natural areas and Kentucky native flora. The significant contribution of private individuals in the protection of natural areas is being recognized and supported by some government programs and tax incentives, but, for the most part, the ultimate conservation tool is landowners who respect the natural areas and rare plants on their properties.

Another aspect of native plant conservation is regulation. The Kentucky legislature enacted the Rare Plant Recognition Act in 1994, which focuses attention on the protection of endangered and threatened plants in Kentucky, one of eight states in the country that had not done so, according to the Center for Wildlife Law (1996). The Kentucky law states: "The General Assembly finds and declares that it is the policy of the Commonwealth to recognize endangered and threatened species of plants for human enjoyment, for scientific purposes, and to ensure their perpetuation as viable components of their ecosystems for the benefit of the people of Kentucky" (Kentucky, State of, 1994). The purpose of this act is to establish an official list of endangered and threatened plants of Kentucky. This first statute, we hope, is a step toward a more comprehensive program for protecting our native flora. For instance, a similar Tennessee law includes some safeguards against poaching rare plants and places limits on the sale of endangered species.

In the meantime, botanists, conservationists, and concerned citizens are getting impatient. Kentucky glade cress, a tiny plant with a global range of northern Bullitt and southern Jefferson counties, provides an example of how the loss of native habitat translates into the loss of species. In recent field surveys, we found that 25 percent of the populations of this Kentucky plant have been eliminated and 74 percent have declined in quality. The primary reason is pressure from devel-

Kentucky glade cress populations are declining as a result of habitat loss.

opment, much of which resulted from a new exit on I-65 that made this area more accessible. The new exit was the first in a succession of changes, including the construction of subdivisions, waterlines, and roads. Bullitt County is one of the fastest growing in the state because of its proximity to Louisville. Who doesn't want a nice house in the country with access to the city? Visiting place after place where the land has been changed and Kentucky glade cress eliminated brings home the message that the demise of our natural lands and, along with them, their native flora and fauna is becoming critically important to environmental health. Kentucky's natural heritage is truly in jeopardy.

Reasons for Decline of Native Species

Humans and all our activities are the primary reason for the decline in natural habitat and the loss of plants worldwide. Consider these simple statistics for the nation from the National Association of Home Builders: the average-size home in this country has more than doubled from 1,100 square feet in 1950 to 2,340 square feet in 2005, and the average occupancy has declined from 3.2 to 2.6 residents in the period from 1969 to 2001. Add to this increase in house size the increase in the number of vehicles per household, from 1.6 to 1.9 during the same period. Our population is around 300 million, and we have 233 million vehicles, according to several governmental reports. The Energy Information Administration estimates the United States has less than 5 percent of the global population, yet we consume 25 percent of world's consumer goods. We consume 33 percent of all the electricity produced in the world. We use 43 percent of the world's gasoline supplies. We produce 25 percent of all the greenhouse gases, a culprit in global climate change, in the world. Several governmental agencies estimate that since 1950 our consumptive lifestyle has resulted in an increase in water use by 127 percent, coal use by 128 percent, and wood use by 171 percent, and our use of energy per individual has more than tripled. Is it any wonder that natural areas and native plants are under siege?

The preeminent biologist E. O. Wilson in his 2002 book, *The Future of Life*, summarized the factors that are causing the declines in native species with the acronym HIPPO, short for Habitat Loss Invasive Species Pollution People Overcollection.

Habitat Loss

Habitat loss is the most serious threat to endangered species and the native flora. In Kentucky from 1992 to 1997, an estimated 130 acres per day were converted for development, according to the Natural Resource and Conservation Service and Iowa State University (2000). For a period in the 1980s and 1990s, Kentucky was developing land faster than all but two other states in the nation. In addition to its effecting the outright loss of habitat, development is being planned with no thought to minimizing its effects on the remaining natural areas, which results in additional indirect impacts. Rarely is the protection of natural resources and natural areas included in zoning plans for an area.

Habitat fragmentation is part of this problem as well. As habitats are divided into smaller pieces, populations (reproducing groups of plants or animals) of species also become divided. Small, isolated populations cannot exchange genetic material and tend to be more vulnerable to extinction. The more diminished the population size, the more easily it is affected by other natural factors like drought and disease. Consider the example of a plant that depends on floral display to attract insects for pollination. As the population becomes smaller, the

Braun's rock-cress is threatened by invasive exotic plants.

Royal catchfly populations are in trouble because of habitat fragmentation.

Changes in natural hydrology are one reason for the decline of Virginia spiraea.

number of plants may not be sufficient to draw the attention of insects or birds, and fewer individual plants are pollinated. If plants are not pollinated, they cannot produce the next generation of seed. One example is the decline of the royal catchfly, a plant that is pollinated largely by hummingbirds. Not only is its habitat being eliminated and fragmented, but the quality of that habitat is also being degraded, which makes it uninhabitable for many native species. Many factors contribute to the degradation of habitat, such as poor logging practices, dams, changes in the hydrology (both surface water and groundwater), and innumerable other disruptions of the natural cycles and processes that contribute to ecosystem stability.

Invasive Exotic Species

Exotic pest plants are becoming so pervasive that this threat is now ranked second only to habitat loss in causing species extinction and could eventually overtake it. Invasive exotic organisms have been introduced, some accidentally and

autumn olive
winged euonymus, burning bush
winter creeper
bush honeysuckle
Miscanthus
kudzu
tree-of-heaven
garlic mustard
musk thistle
oriental bittersweet
poison hemlock
crown vetch
Chinese yam

*for full list visit www.se-eppc.org/ky

American chestnut declined because of an invasive exotic pathogen.

some intentionally, for horticulture, agriculture, erosion control, or wildlife habitat. These biological scourges can replace a diverse and stable flora and eventually undermine an ecosystem. Some of Kentucky's most dangerous threats are bush honeysuckle, garlic mustard, and Japanese grass. Do you have burning bush in your yard? Or winter creeper? Many homes come with four or more exotic pest plants already in the landscape because they have been so commonly used. These plants become ticking time bombs waiting for some event to allow them a foothold in a natural area, where they explode in abundance. Many are dispersed by birds and do not even need disturbance; they can be found deep in the interior of a stable natural area. Eventually, these pests replace the natural flora and disrupt the natural relationships with fauna, the result being a disabled ecosystem.

Pest animals and diseases are also a menacing prospect for Kentucky's native flora. Hemlock woolly adelgid, emerald ash borer, and oak wilt are a few of the most imminent. The threat of an eastern Kentucky without hemlocks looms as the woolly adelgid enters the state from Virginia. A previous generation watched all the majestic American chestnuts succumb to a nonindigenous fungus, which still prevents these trees from regaining dominance over the forest canopy.

Pollution

Whether water, air, or noise, pollution can be harmful not only to other species but also to the mammals we care about the most—ourselves. In this case, species loss can be a symptom of problems that also directly affect people's health. Buchmann and Nabhan in *The Forgotten Pollinators* (1996) remind us that pollution can cause pollinators, mostly insects, to decline, which affects agriculture and native flora, including rare plants. The lack of visitation by pollinators is at crisis proportions for agriculture in some parts of the country and has also been blamed for lack of seed set in prairie flora and endangered plants.

People

There is an ever-increasing number of people, and this is straining natural resources around the world. In addition, home gardening and even recreation can affect rare plants. For example, rare plants and other organisms that occur along cliff lines, such as the white-haired goldenrod in the Red River Gorge, are trampled by people who hike, camp, or climb rocks. Similarly, off-road recreational vehicles and horse trails can cause erosion, invite weeds into natural areas, and change the hydrology. All these effects lead to declines in rare plants.

Gardeners are becoming savvier about avoiding exotic pest plants and using plants native to Kentucky, which may reduce the incidence of pests like insects and fungus in gardens and the amount of water needed to sustain them. The key to the use of natives in landscaping is to choose species that are wide-

White-haired goldenrod is threatened by people trampling them along cliff lines.

Thread-foot occurs only in very pure, free-flowing streams and is threatened by pollution.

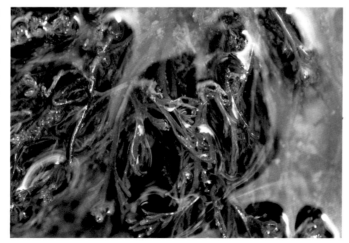

Kentucky lady's-slipper is a species that collectors and gardeners dig from the wild.

spread in Kentucky and native to the region where they are being used. There are also many nonnative cultivated plants that are not invasive. With a little information, it is possible to avoid plant species that could cause harm to natural areas.

Overcollection

Collection of native plants from the wild is increasing for the pharmaceutical trade (including herbal medicines) as well as for other uses, such as florist materials (moss harvest), wreath making (vine collection), and gardening. Some of the most vulnerable rare plants are orchids, trilliums, aquatic plants, and a few mints. People with a "sackful of Kentucky lady's-slipper root" who inquire about the legal restrictions on the sale of this species are not interested in transplanting; these orchids were dug with the intention of selling for herbal preparations. There are laws restricting international trade of any orchid and other specifically listed plants under the Convention on International Trade of Endangered Species (CITES). Federally listed species are protected from interstate sale as well. Though these laws are helpful, a population of Kentucky lady's-slipper that is dug for transplanting to a local yard is no less destroyed than one that is dug for resale. Again, an informed buyer can avoid supporting indiscriminate wild collecting that harms Kentucky's natural areas.

Will education be enough to protect Kentucky's native flora from these myriad threats? What does it take to incorporate conservation and reverence for Kentucky's natural heritage into industries, businesses, and culture? The wilds of Bullitt

County again provide an example of the conflict between culture and nature. Kentucky glade cress populations have persisted in the yards of homes in this area that were formerly natural glades, their conservation value now minimal. Eventually, these lawn sites will be lost to the landowner's struggle to have a grassy yard despite the surface rock and poor soils for turf—soils perfect for glade cress. Another rare species of these glades, Eggleston's violet, occurs as splashes of purple among the patches of white glade cress. Once while talking to a landowner about looking for the Eggleston's violet near her yard and how unusual this violet is, I could see she was not buying it. When I paused for breath, she looked at me and said, "Oh, violets, violets! I think there are violets on the moon!" I caught her on a day when she was in the fierce throes of battle with weedy violets in her yard. Conservation of rare plants is a struggle between people and nature. It is about finding a way to have a yard without costing Kentucky's wilderness. More to the point, it is about whether Kentucky's natural heritage is valued enough before it is too late to save.

Eggleston's violet, a species of special concern, occurs on limestone glades.

Reasons for Protecting Native Plants

Native plants are an ideal group of organisms to showcase the importance of protecting native organisms and systems: there are direct economic and social impacts that occur from the use of native plants for such things as pharmaceuticals and agricultural commodities. Generally speaking, the importance of protecting plants falls under two broad categories, extrinsic and intrinsic values. The list below is a modification of Natureserve's list of reasons to protect biodiversity.

REASONS TO PROTECT RARE PLANTS

Intrinsic
Caring for creation (moral and ethical reasons)
Beauty of the natural world (aesthetic and cultural reasons)
Creative and informative beasts: humans (educational and scientific reasons)

Extrinsic
Economic wealth of nature (economic reasons)
Feeding people (agricultural reasons)
Nature's medicine cabinet (pharmaceuticals)
Life-support system (ecosystem services)

First presented are the reasons that biodiversity in general, and native plants specifically, has value, regardless of the benefit to humans. Intrinsic values include the moral and ethical reasons for protecting the natural world, the inherent worth of any organism. Extrinsic values are utilitarian or practical values and include such things as food, medicines, natural products, fiber, and so on. These values are easy to highlight and show a direct contribution to humans. It is hard not to accept the extrinsic values of plants because 40 percent of our medicines are derived from plants, and about 20 species of plants basically feed the world.

From a moral or ethical perspective, protecting the natural world can be wrapped up in a single statement: it is the right thing to do. "Caring for creation" is the moral basis for protecting the diversity of life; this concept lies within each major faith or ethical system throughout the world. Almost every faith community or religion has a statement about caring for the earth and being good stewards. For example, the Dalai Lama, a leader of the Buddhist faith, writes: "Our planet is our house, and we must keep it in order and take care of it if we are genuinely concerned about happiness for ourselves, our children, our friends, and other sentient beings who share this great house with us."

Hindus also think of the earth as their home and consider its preservation a devotion of love; they envision catastrophic repercussions for exploiting the land. Muslim interpretations of the Koran speak to our responsibility to use our knowledge of the earth to maintain a balance that exists in the environment.

The Christian premise behind this intrinsic value is that if God created the heavens and the earth as well as humans, it follows that all life is sacred and has intrinsic value. The late Pope John Paul II stated in his World Day of Peace address in 1990: "On another level, delicate ecological balances are upset by the uncontrolled destruction of animal and plant life or by a reckless exploitation of natural resources. It should be pointed out that all of this, even if carried out in the name of progress and well-being, is ultimately to mankind's disadvantage. . . . Today the ecological crisis has assumed such proportions as to be the responsibility of everyone. . . . I wish to repeat that the ecological crisis is a moral issue." The basis for this moral responsibility lies in Judeo-Christian scripture; it is stated six times in the first 25 chapters of the book of Genesis that creation is good, and the idea that humans must be good environmental stewards is referred to more than 100 times throughout both the Old and New Testaments.

Closely related to intrinsic value is the noneconomic value that species provide, and this is closely related to spiritual, cultural, and aesthetic values. This value is appropriately titled "the beauty of the natural world." Once again, Pope John Paul II tied this value to religion when he stated, "Our very contact with nature has a deep restorative power; contemplation of its magnificence imparts peace and serenity." Though there may be religious overtones to this connection with nature, there are also secular viewpoints: for example, people look to the natural world as a source of inspiration and beauty, as preeminent scientists such as Stephen Kellert and Edward O. Wilson report in their books *The Value of Life* and the *Biophilia Hypothesis.* This point is corroborated by other scientists, who have found that humans value individual species for their beauty, rarity, complexity, and adaptations. Have you read a children's book lately? Just look at the myriad titles, and you will find that animals, plants, and nature in general provide much of the inspiration for these books. It is hard to imagine art without the inspiration of nature, whether it is the flower paintings of Georgia O'Keeffe, the landscapes of Jean-Baptiste-Camille Corot, or the photography of Ansel Adams. The plants showcased in this book are a perfect example of the splendor nature has to offer and why we should protect plants for their beauty alone.

This beauty of nature moves us from the intrinsic to the extrinsic values (we will discuss the final intrinsic value, educational and scientific reasons, a bit later): one of the big reasons for protecting biodiversity is "the economic wealth of nature." Beauty, inspiration, and awe are the basis for one economic effect: tourism, particularly ecotourism. One recent study estimated the annual recreational value of natural resources at a staggering $800 billion. If you look at just one country, Costa Rica, which has embraced all aspects of ecotourism, and contemplate that in the past two decades ecotourism has generated more income than its leading export crop, bananas, you see the economic significance of protecting nature. Closer to home, we found that in a 2001 U.S. Fish and Wildlife Service study, the national wildlife refuges in the southeastern United States had more than 11 million visitors, which resulted in the creation of more than 8,500 jobs and generation of more than $451 million in economic activity. The 2001 national survey of fish, wildlife, and wildlife-associated recreation found that in Kentucky more than 1.5 million people participated in wildlife-watching activities and spent an estimated $8.1 million on trip-related expenses and another $5.4 million in equipment purchases. There is a very real economic incentive for protecting the natural world.

The economic effect goes beyond ecotourism to providing materials for commercial products, agriculture, and medicine. The list of commercial products that derive some of their ingredients from native plants (excluding food and medicine, which will be dealt with separately) is long indeed. It includes soaps, shampoos, paints, paper, vinyl, polishes, deodorants, dyes, fire-extinguisher foams, sunscreens, wood and wood products, cork, rubber, pencil erasers, plastics, nail-polish removers, glues, and lotions. The jojoba plant that occurs in American southwestern deserts provides one example. This plant contains a liquid wax that is taking the place of the oil of the sperm whale, a declining and protected species, as an industrial lubricant. A recent study found that the market for natural products, those produced largely from natural ingredients, is an amazing $87 billion a year.

A second factor is "feeding people": plants provide food for the world, and biodiversity is important to healthy crops—a good reason to protect biodiversity. We all need to eat, and throughout human history we have eaten more than 12,000 different kinds of native plants. Sadly, today roughly 20 species of plants feed the world, and the big three are in the grass family: rice, corn, and wheat. But think of all the other native plants that have been cultivated to provide diversity to the diet: blueberries, cranberries, blackberries, raspberries, currants, grapes, and so on. Also, native species may be used to bolster immunity in cultivated plants, and they may be both culturally and economically significant. A rare species in Kentucky, the northern fox grape, is the progenitor of the cultivated Concord grape, which can be eaten fresh, preserved in jelly, or used to make wine. Kentucky was "the grape capital of the United States" before Prohibition. There was an outbreak of *Phylloxera vitifoliae*, an aphidlike louse, in the late 1800s in

Northern fox grape (fruit and foliage) is a species of special concern. The genetic material from this species helped save the wine industry.

Europe, and European winemakers then imported American grape rootstock. Their wine industry was saved with genetic material from four native North American grape species, including our own northern fox grape.

In addition to fruits, think of the nuts, sunflower seeds, squashes, beans, maple syrup, and all the other foodstuffs that are derived from native plants. But the big economic impact is from commercial agriculture. One example highlights the importance of native plants in providing genetic diversity to strengthen our food supply. In 1970 a leaf fungus destroyed approximately 15 percent of the U.S. corn crop, which had an estimated value of $2 billion. Corn is susceptible to several other viruses, and it was the use of teosinte, the closest native relative to our corn plant, that salvaged commercial corn production. Through breeding and hybridizing genetic material from this primitive corn plant, four blight-resistant varieties were developed that allowed the continued cultivation of this staple food item in North America. In 2005 the value of

Canada yew is listed as threatened. A closely related species provided the basis for an important anticancer drug.

has two compounds, vinblastine and vincristine, that are used to treat acute lymphoma and Hodgkin's disease. Think about how many lives have been saved and the fact that these drugs contribute $180 million annually to the U.S. economy.

There is yet another economic factor dependent on native plants and animals, and it is not directly quantifiable but extremely important nonetheless. We will call it an indirect economic value or, more appropriately, our "life-support system." In essence, these are the ecosystem services that provide clean air and water, global climate regulation, soil and water protection, plant pollination and dispersal, and nutrient cycling. Unfortunately, these "products" are not obvious to the average person and have not traditionally been valued by economists. That is changing, however, and two recent studies highlight the economic value of our life-support system. One study in the late 1990s attempted to measure the economic value of ecosystem services and found it was worth twice the global GNP, or $33 trillion. Another study found that the ability of tropical rain forests to absorb global carbon dioxide is worth $46 billion.

Some plants also provide information about the health of natural communities in much the same way canaries once warned coal miners of unhealthy air in the mines. The kinds of plants and animals that thrive—or not—in rivers and streams provide warnings about water quality; those that are sensitive disappear from waterways. The flora and fauna of every habitat tell the story of land use at that site and predict what we can expect with more degradation of their natural communities.

There is no question that biodiversity inspires creativity and helps us solve problems through science. Did you know that Velcro was inspired by the lowly cocklebur plant, which sticks to people's clothing? Or that bats were important study animals used to help develop navigational aids for blind peo-

the corn crop in Kentucky was estimated at $336 million, and our state accounts for only 1.8 percent of the corn production in the United States.

Almost as essential as "feeding people" is "nature's medicine cabinet." It has been estimated that 80 percent of the world's population uses plants as a source of pharmaceuticals, another reason to protect native flora. An amazing 40 percent of all prescription medications sold in the United States are derived from some native plant, animal, or microorganism, and 57 percent of the top 150 prescribed medications are derived from these same species. The list of these pharmaceuticals is large and includes such things as aspirin, penicillin, digitoxin, L-dopa, Taxol, quinine, and others. Consider the simple example of the rosy periwinkle. Scientists found that this little plant ple? Or that a halobacteria, bacteria that are adapted to high-salt environments and that thrive in the San Francisco Bay, could hold the key to revolutionizing computer fiber optics? These are but a few of the examples of how we increase our knowledge by studying native plants and animals.

Humans have been studying nature for hundreds of years, yet we are still largely ignorant about how many natural systems work. We get insights here and there and can piece together theories, but we are still, for instance, largely unable to predict how the loss of any individual species will affect the entire ecosystem The classic metaphor is a spider web, an intricate and well-designed system that is held together by a series of distinct points. Think of the points as individual species and the threads as ecological functions. How many species or functions can be removed before the entire web collapses? We still don't have the answer.

Natural Communities of Kentucky

All native plants have adapted to particular habitats, or natural communities. They are tied to the environmental and ecological conditions that created that community, whether it is hemlock forests, sandstone cliffs, or stream terraces. Spiked blazing-star lives in dry prairies. Wild ginger lives in mesic forests. Rare plants also live in a variety of natural communities. Some, such as large-leaf grass-of-parnassus, require very specific conditions found only in a single rare community, a particular type of wetland. Others, such as showy gentian, occur in common mesic to dry forest communities in eastern Kentucky. To understand Kentucky's rare plants better, it is necessary to know about natural communities and where they occur. To protect rare plants and native plant diversity, it is necessary to protect the natural communities and the processes that support ecosystems.

Natural communities are groupings of specific plants and animals (along with accompanying organisms such as fungi, bacteria, and other microorganisms) that live together under a specific range of environmental conditions (soil, moisture, light) and are repeated across the landscape wherever these conditions occur. They are classified by the dominant and characteristic plants or by physical characteristics of the site, such as geology, soils, and hydrology—or by both.

Difference in type of soil or bedrock results in a change or shift in the dominant species and other plants, which results

ECOLOGICAL DEFINITIONS

Below are several words used repeatedly to explain the character of natural communities or plant distributions and conditions.

Biodiversity: all living things and the natural processes that sustain them.

Disjunct: disconnected from one another; that is, in two or more different places.

Endemic: characteristic of a defined area, native.

Extirpated: eliminated, extinct.

Mesic or mesophytic: characterized by or requiring a moderate amount of moisture.

Xeric: very dry, requiring only a small amount of moisture.

in a change in the natural community. The dry forests on limestone have different floras from those on sandstone. The physical conditions in shale and limestone glades are very similar —but some of the plants are different because the soils and geology differ. These differences create natural variation and increase biodiversity among communities, even among those that are similar.

When ecological conditions, such as soil or hydrology, are changed, the community changes as the plants and other organisms react to the new conditions. If the conditions that supported the original community have changed enough, the community that develops at that site is not the same as the original. As the Kentucky landscape has been used for logging and grazing, for instance, natural communities, even widespread, common ones such as dry oak forests, have often been degraded or damaged beyond recovery. A result of this community degradation is the reduction of plant abundance and diversity; plants have been eliminated by the disturbances and are unable to reestablish themselves. High-quality natural plant communities, even of the most common types, are very rare today.

At the time of European settlement, the middle of the eighteenth century, Kentucky looked considerably different from the way it looks today. Although the flora, fauna, and natural communities were not well documented as the state became settled, historic journals and literature provide a glimpse into the ecological past and help create a fairly good picture of what the land cover was like. Most of Kentucky was covered in a seemingly endless old-growth forest that stretched from the Cumberland Mountains in the extreme southeast to the Mississippi River along the western border. It is estimated that 85 to 90 percent of Kentucky was forested. This vast forest ranged from lowland bald cypress swamps to rich mesic (moist) upland forests, to xeric (very dry), stunted post-oak forests, to high-elevation northern hardwood forests. But not all Kentucky was forested. Large areas of prairie and woodland occurred, especially in the western half of the state. In addition, smaller but no less important communities, such as seeps and glades, were scattered throughout the state.

Some areas of forest were cleared by Native Americans for farming, but these were primarily restricted to the larger river bottoms. Native Americans also used fire as a tool to manipulate their environment. Although we can speculate on how much effect Native Americans had on their environment, there is no question that the scale and severity were minor compared to the environmental impacts of humans today.

Natural Regions of Kentucky

A brief description of the natural regions of Kentucky is necessary to understand the distribution of natural communities, as well as the flora and fauna within the state. There are three major physiographic provinces in the state: the Coastal Plain, the Interior Low Plateaus, and the Appalachian Highlands.

In the west are the Mississippi Alluvial Plain and East Gulf Coastal Plain sections of the Coastal Plain province. These areas are the youngest in the state, having been covered by ocean as recently as 60 million years ago. The lowest point in Kentucky, 257 feet above sea level, is in Fulton County, along the Mississippi River in the southwest corner of the state. Much of this area is flat to rolling and is covered in loess (wind-blown silt) or alluvium (soil deposited by floods); many of Kentucky's wetlands are in this region. There were also large prairies here at the time of settlement.

Moving eastward, the Interior Low Plateaus province begins with the Shawnee Hills, a region with a series of layers of Mississippian and Pennsylvanian sandstones, limestones, and shales that have eroded into hills and caves in some parts, and flat, poorly drained areas in other parts. Most of the Shawnee Hills was forested, but the area also contained prairies and woodlands. Extensive wetlands occupied lowlands in the interior.

The Highland Rim is underlain primarily by Mississippian limestone and is relatively flat to rolling, although some areas are very hilly. Some parts, especially the Pennyroyal Plain subsection, have developed extensive karst topography: they contain hundreds of sinkholes, caves, and subterranean streams.

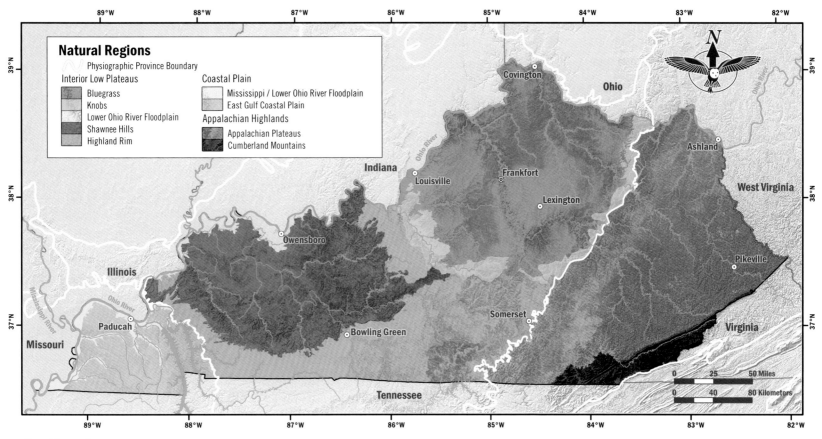

Natural Regions

Interior Low Plateaus
- Bluegrass
- Knobs
- Lower Ohio River Floodplain
- Shawnee Hills
- Highland Rim

Coastal Plain
- Mississippi / Lower Ohio River Floodplain
- East Gulf Coastal Plain

Appalachian Highlands
- Appalachian Plateaus
- Cumberland Mountains

Physiographic Province Boundary

Greg Abernathy, KSNPC

In the mid-eighteenth century, large prairies occurred in this section, especially in the Pennyroyal and Elizabethtown Karst Plain subsections. The eastern part of the Highland Rim was primarily forested. Swamp forests and marshes were limited to small to large depressions and flat, poorly drained upland areas.

Moving northeast, the Bluegrass is part of an eroded dome and contains the oldest exposed rock in Kentucky: Ordovician-, Silurian-, and Devonian-aged limestones and shales. At the

time of settlement, most of the Bluegrass was forested, but some areas were open woodland or open, grassy woods. The Knobs is a relatively narrow area of isolated hills, ridges, and intervening flats that forms a horseshoe-shaped ring around the outer edge of the Bluegrass. Besides the forests, there were small prairies and glades.

The Appalachian Highlands, made up of the Appalachian Plateaus and Cumberland Mountains, is the most rugged part of the state and has the greatest relief as well as the highest

Oak-hickory forest is the most common forest type in Kentucky.

elevations in Kentucky. The plateaus are, for the most part, highly dissected, the result being steep hills and narrow valleys. The Cumberland Mountains are the largest and only true mountains in Kentucky, having been folded and upthrusted. Black Mountain, in Harlan County, has the highest elevation in the state at 4,145 feet above sea level. This region was and still is heavily forested.

Upland Forested Communities

Today Kentucky is less than 50 percent forested; most forests occur as small woodlots and not as large, contiguous tracts. The forests of today bear little resemblance to the old-growth forests that once towered over the landscape. Today's forests bear the scars of many decades of abuse. Repeated logging, overgrazing, and too many fires have taken a sad toll. Add to that the decimation of one of the most important trees in Kentucky, the American chestnut, by an imported fungus.

Forests are communities with a canopy cover greater than 75 percent, in which little direct sunlight reaches the ground during the growing season. Most of Kentucky's forests are temperate deciduous forests: their trees lose their leaves in the autumn and go dormant during the winter. Kentucky also has areas of evergreen forests of pine, hemlock, or cedar. Forests can be all-deciduous, all-evergreen, or mixed.

Kentucky is rich in forest communities. The climate, geology, soils, and topography create a mosaic of conditions that support a wide variety of forest types. Upland forest communities can be generally divided into dry and mesic forests.

(far left) A pine-oak community with mountain laurel flowering in the foreground.

(near left) Appalachian mesophytic forests are some of the most diverse temperate deciduous forests in the world.

Dry forests. Dry (subxeric) forests are common in Kentucky and can be found anywhere there are poor, rocky, thin, or very well-drained soils, especially on narrow ridgetops and south- and west-facing slopes. Most of these forests are deciduous but may have evergreen pines and cedars, especially in the driest areas. Oaks and hickories are characteristic of these forests. The typical trees of the dry forests can include white oak, black oak, chestnut oak, scarlet oak, southern red oak, chinkapin oak, pignut hickory, shagbark hickory, red maple, and sourwood. The driest sites with the poorest soil can also have post oaks and blackjack oaks.

A type of dry forest, the **Appalachian oak forest**, occurs commonly in the hills and mountains of eastern Kentucky. It is dominated by chestnut oak with scarlet oak, black oak, black gum, and red maple, often with a dense understory of mountain laurel. Other characteristic plants include trailing arbutus and spotted wintergreen. Before its demise, the American chestnut was a common constituent of this forest type.

Mesic forests. Mesic forests occur throughout Kentucky in moister and richer areas than the dry forests. They grow where soil is deeper and in protected areas like ravines and hollows and on north- and east-facing slopes. These are the forests where spring wildflowers put on their best display. Mesic for-

Catawba rhododendron flowers in the dry Appalachian oak forest on Pine Mountain in southeastern Kentucky.

ests of eastern Kentucky have the greatest number of species—diversity tends to decline as one moves west in the state.

Typical canopy trees in the mesic forests include sugar maple, American beech, white ash, white oak, red oak, tulip tree, black walnut, bitternut hickory, and shagbark hickory. Understory trees and shrubs include spicebush, pawpaw, and wild hydrangea. Typical wildflowers are trillium, bloodroot, wood poppy, and jack-in-the-pulpit.

A type of mesic forest, the **Bluegrass mesophytic cane forest**, occurs in the Inner Bluegrass region. Historically it had much native giant cane in the understory. Today only degraded remnants remain. It is dominated by sugar maple, black walnut, Ohio buckeye, and Shumard's oak.

The **Appalachian mesophytic forest** of the Cumberland Mountains and Appalachian Plateaus is the richest expression of the mesophytic forests. It has a higher diversity of tree species than all other types of temperate forests in North America and is one of only a few rich, temperate forests on Earth. This richness can also be seen in the diversity of the mosses, liverworts, lichens, ferns, wildflowers, shrubs, and vines.

A great variety of tree species can make up the canopy in this type of forest, and any one forest's exact composition depends on many factors. In 1950 E. Lucy Braun, a famous forest ecologist, listed 38 species of trees that occur in the mixed mesophytic forest of eastern Kentucky. Common trees of this forest include those listed for the mesic forest, as well as (among many others) eastern hemlock, white pine, cucumber magnolia, black gum, black cherry, and sweet birch. Trees that are considered indicators of the mixed mesophytic forest are yellow buckeye, white basswood, and yellow birch. Understory trees and shrubs are also diverse: such species as wild hydrangea, buffalo nut, sweet pepperbush, northern spicebush, bladdernut, pawpaw, and viburnum occur. Vines include Virginia creeper, pipe-vine, crossvine, and grape. The groundcover is also rich and diverse, with many ferns and wildflowers.

A unique and rare forest type in Kentucky is the **Cumberland highlands forest**. It is a type of northern hardwood forest and occurs only in the Cumberland Mountains at elevations greater than 3,400 feet above sea level. It is more similar to hardwood forests of the northeastern United States than to any other forest in Kentucky. It primarily occurs on Kentucky's tallest mountain, Black Mountain in Harlan County, but small examples of it can be found on a few other high spots. Because of high precipitation (more than 60 inches per year) and cooler temperatures due to elevation (4,145 feet above sea level), this forest is extremely rich and lush and supports a diverse and showy assemblage of wildflowers. Characteristic trees include yellow birch, black cherry, sugar maple, and yellow buckeye.

Another unusual type of forest is the **xero-hydric flatwoods.** This uncommon community occurs on flat sites that have a fragipan, a layer of clay beneath the surface that restricts downward water movement. This results in soil that is saturated with water in the winter and spring but then dries out in the summer and fall, creating extremely dry conditions. This wet-dry cycle creates unusual growing conditions in which wetland plants like pin and overcup oaks and xerophytic plants like blazing-star and rushfoil grow together. Historically, the more open conditions of this community were probably maintained by periodic fires.

Upland Nonforested Communities

Prairies, glades, and woodlands, open to partially wooded communities, occupied up to 10 to 15 percent of Kentucky at the time of settlement in the mid-eighteenth century. Fire and grazing by bison, elk, and deer were important factors in maintaining the open conditions. Today these communities are very rare and occur only as scattered remnants owing primarily to habitat destruction, but fire suppression is also an important cause.

In Kentucky, glades are uncommon and rarely large. Many are only an acre or two, and others are much smaller. They occur scattered throughout the state where bedrock is near the surface or exposed. This creates extreme environmental conditions, and most of the plants either are very drought tolerant or are annuals that flower and set seed before the heat of the summer. The harshest habitat, bare rock, will not support vascular plants; lichens and mosses are most common.

Woody plants do not grow well under these conditions, and these areas are naturally open. Some small trees and shrubs, especially red cedar, grow in cracks in the rocks or in pockets of deeper soil. Other woody plants that can grow in or around the edges of glades include post oak, blackjack oak, winged elm, fragrant sumac, and redbud.

Sandstone glades occur in the Shawnee Hills and the Cumberland Plateau. **Limestone glades** occur primarily in the Highland Rim (Mississippian Plateau) but also in the Outer Bluegrass and Knobs. **Dolomite** (a type of limestone) **glades** are restricted to the western Outer Bluegrass. **Shale glades** occur primarily in the Knobs region, where Mississippian, Silurian, and Devonian shales are exposed.

Limestone glades occur on slopes and on flat-bedded outcrops, often called pavement bedrock. Glades on slopes are very well drained and droughty. Flat glades, on the other hand, are often saturated or even flooded in the winter and spring, which creates a unique growing condition that only certain plants are adapted to. As might be expected, this is habitat for several rare plants. Characteristic grasses of limestone glades include poverty dropseed, tall dropseed, little bluestem, and three-awn grass. Typical forbs include prickly-pear cactus,

Pine Creek barrens, Bullitt County, is a mosaic of woodland, glade, and prairie communities.

pale purple coneflower, widow's-cross, heliotrope, small skull-cap, and false aloe.

Sandstone glades often have large expanses of lichens and moss-covered bedrock. Curly grass, broomsedge, and little bluestem are common in scattered pockets of soil. Typical flowering plants include rushfoil, golden-aster, greater tickseed, round-fruited Saint-John's-wort, orange-grass, narrow-leaf pinweed, sandwort, Virginia dwarf-dandelion, and forked blue-curls.

Shale glades are often small and usually occur on steep slopes. The shale-covered slope is unstable, and loose shale fragments cover the ground, slowly creeping down the slope. This affords a poor habitat for plants, or even lichens and mosses, to get established. Therefore, shale glades have the least diversity or plant cover of all the glades. Often scattered around the shale openings are gnarly chestnut oaks and a few Virginia pine and redbuds that always appear to be half dead. Some of the tough herbaceous plants that can survive these places include curly grass, wild pink, and forked chickweed. Interestingly, no rare plants have been found in shale glades in Kentucky, but several rare plants occur in such conditions in Virginia and West Virginia.

Prairies are grasslands dominated by native grasses and forbs and contain less than 25 percent cover of trees. In the mid-eighteenth century, Kentucky had an estimated 2.5 to 3 million acres of prairie, mostly in the Highland Rim (Pennyroyal Plain) and Coastal Plain (Jackson Purchase) regions of the state. Other, smaller areas of prairie occurred in scattered localities. Early accounts describe vast prairie areas that were 60 to 70 miles long and 60 miles wide, with tall grasses and hardly a tree or shrub to be seen. The early settlers who came upon the huge grasslands called them "barrens" because they

Limestone flat-rock glade communities have exposed rock and shallow soils and harbor numerous rare species.

Tall-grass prairie (with state endangered royal catchfly) once covered hundreds of thousands of acres in Kentucky. Today only scattered remnants remain.

were treeless, and they thought the soil was poor. The largest prairie remnant in Kentucky, and one of the largest in the eastern United States, is on Fort Campbell in southern Christian County. Other than that, only a few thousand acres are left, in widely scattered and mostly degraded remnants.

Prairies require periodic fires to restrict invasion of trees and shrubs. It is thought that Native Americans burned the grasslands primarily to promote new growth to aid in attracting game animals to hunt. Natural lightning also caused fires. Grazing by large herds of ungulates also helped maintain the grasslands.

Prairies range from wet to moist to dry. **Wet prairies** are a type of wetland and occur in areas with deep, poorly drained soils and are dominated by cord grass, along with gama-grass, switchgrass, and big bluestem, all of which grow up to nine feet tall. Typical wildflowers in the wet prairie include narrow-leaved sunflower, cardinal-flower, and sweet coneflower.

Mesic prairies are the typical tall-grass prairies that were repeatedly mentioned by the first settlers. The grasses can be almost as tall as a man on horseback. Big bluestem and Indian grass are the dominant species, but other grasses are also present. **Dry prairies** occur over limestone or sandstone on sites that are rockier and have thinner, droughty soil. These dry prairies are often called mid-grass prairies because the grasses do not get as tall as in the wet and mesic prairies. The most common grass in the dry prairie is little bluestem. Others include dropseed, Indian grass, Elliott's broomsedge, and three-awn grass. A great diversity of wildflowers grows in the least disturbed prairie remnants. These include blazing-stars, purple and yellow coneflower, large-leaf wild indigo, sunflowers, prairie dock, tall tickseed, and goldenrods.

Woodlands are partially wooded communities that have a canopy cover of 25 to 75 percent. In other words, it is not completely open like a prairie but is not closed like a forest. Usually some kind of periodic disturbance, such as fire, drought, or grazing, is needed to maintain the open structure. This lack of a closed canopy permits much more sunlight to reach the ground, allowing prairie and other sun-loving plants to grow.

In the mid-eighteenth century, there was a considerable amount of woodland in Kentucky, although it was most prevalent in the western half of the state. Today natural woodlands are rare because of habitat destruction or lack of fire. Most woodland communities occur on dry sites, but some occur in more mesic situations.

Pine and pine-oak woodlands occur sporadically in eastern Kentucky in the Appalachian Plateaus and Cumberland Mountains and in the Knobs region. A few of these woodlands also occur in the Shawnee Hills in western Kentucky. In eastern Kentucky the pine woodlands can be dominated by Virginia pine, pitch pine, shortleaf pine, or, more rarely, a combination. In the western part of the state, Virginia pine dominates.

A very rare type of woodland that is essentially extirpated now is the **Bluegrass savanna-woodland**, known to occur only in the Bluegrass region. It is thought that grazing by large herds of bison, elk, and deer, as well as infrequent fire, maintained the open, savanna-like appearance that was so appealing to the early settlers. The exact composition and extent of this community is not known because the Bluegrass region was the earliest settled and the natural landscape was altered before it was well documented. The Bluegrass savanna-woodland was dominated by huge, spreading bur oaks, chinkapin oaks, and blue ash, some of which can still be seen standing guard in the famous Bluegrass horse pastures.

The **xeric calcareous** and **xeric acidic woodlands** are variously called oak barrens, post-oak barrens, cedar barrens, sand-

Griffith Woods, Harrison County, is one of very few remaining examples of Bluegrass savanna-woodland.

stone barrens, and limestone barrens. They are all dominated by oaks that are usually scattered about or in small groves. The ground between the oaks is usually carpeted in sun-loving prairie grasses and forbs. Plants that are less sun tolerant frequently occur in the shade of the trees. These woodlands are often adjacent to prairies or on dry, droughty ground.

Cliff Communities

Towering cliffs and beautifully sculpted rock outcrops add great beauty and interest to the Kentucky landscape. Kentucky has many hundreds of miles of cliffs, some of which are hundreds of feet tall and miles long. Cliffs line many of our rivers and streams and cap many ridges and hills. Like glades, the bare rock and narrow ledges of cliffs and outcrops afford a limited variety of places for plants to live. As a substrate for lichens, mosses, and liverworts, however, they are a veritable paradise; on many cliffs these plants completely cover the rock surface.

Cliffs may also be dry or moist or have water permanently dripping or flowing over the surface. Depending on available moisture and type of rock, alum-roots, Virginia saxifrage, columbine, shooting-star, and sedums are common, as are ferns, including a variety of spleenworts such as Bradley's, lobed, mountain, and maidenhair. Other common ferns are rock polypody, hairy lip, bulblet, Tennessee bladder, and purple and smooth cliffbrake. Some cliffs and outcrops have many vines either climbing up or hanging down. These include poison ivy, trumpet creeper, Virginia creeper, bittersweet, and grapes.

Unique features of some cliffs are rock shelters, also called rockhouses. Rock shelters are eroded areas along cliffs with overhanging rock roofs; they vary from shallow indentations to huge and cavelike, hundreds of feet wide and almost as deep. Some are dry and have almost nothing growing in them, and some have water dripping from the roof or back wall and are covered with liverworts, mosses, and ferns. A number of plants are adapted to the lower light levels in rockhouses. Some characteristic species include pellitory, roundleaf catchfly, meadow-rue, sweet white violet, and clearweed, as well as ferns such as walking, lady, intermediate wood, maidenhair spleenwort, filmy, and bulblet.

Lowland and Wetland Communities

In the middle of the eighteenth century, Kentucky had more than 2.2 million acres of wetlands. Today, more than 80 percent of the wetlands have been drained and destroyed, and the remaining acres, with a few exceptions, are mostly degraded. Wetlands may be forested or nonforested. Forested wetlands range from deepwater cypress and tupelo swamps to infrequently flooded bottomland terrace forests. Nonforested wetlands range from seasonally wet meadows to marshes and shrub swamps.

Forested Wetland Communities

At the wettest end of the spectrum are the swamps and sloughs, dominated by bald cypress and swamp tupelo, either individually or mixed together. These are the classic swamps of the Deep South, with cypress knees rising eerily above the water. Kentucky is near the northern edge of the range of this

Wet limestone ledges with state-listed water stitchwort and wild hyacinth along a stream.

community, and it is restricted to bottomlands in the Eastern Gulf Coastal Plain and Shawnee Hills. The most common shrub in the understory is buttonbush, but swamp rose and Virginia willow are also commonly found. Terrestrial plants that can be found growing epiphytically (growing on other plants) include false nettle, few-branched beggar-ticks, and greater marsh Saint-John's-wort. Other herbaceous plants are either floaters, such as duckweed, or submerged, such as pondweed.

Bottomland hardwood forests are the most common of the forested wetland communities. They occur statewide in the floodplains of rivers and streams. These forests are some of the most productive of all of Kentucky's forests, and many have been cleared and put to agricultural use. Because of the rich alluvial soils and abundant moisture, plants grow faster and the forest supports a high diversity of species. The most common and characteristic trees include sweetgum, American elm, silver maple, green ash, pin oak, red maple, river birch, box elder, black willow, eastern cottonwood, and American sycamore; those in western Kentucky may have willow oak, overcup oak, swamp cottonwood, and pecan as well.

One of the most impressive and rarest of all forest types is the **bottomland hardwood terrace forest**. These forests occur on higher and better-drained soils in the larger floodplains, and as a result they do not flood for as long as the surrounding bottomland forests. Because of this, most of this community has been cleared and used as cropland. Trees in this forest, a mix of bottomland and mesic species, can grow to a huge size.

Uplands can also have wetlands, **depression swamps** and **ponds**, in areas where drainage is slow or impeded, such as depressions or sinkholes. Some of these depressions can be hundreds of acres and hold permanent ponds, whereas others flood for a period and then the water slowly recedes. Also, a version of flatwoods, **wet flatwoods**, occurs in uplands; these stay wet-

A marsh community dominated by emergent aquatic plants, including the state threatened lake cress, in Fulton County.

A deepwater cypress swamp.

ter longer and rarely dry out completely. This uncommon community has cherrybark oak, willow oak, sweetgum, American beech, and green ash, along with other wetland species.

Nonforested Wetland Communities

Nonforested wetland communities include large expanses of bottomland marshes and shrub swamps covering hundreds of acres as well as small upland bogs and seepy cliffs. Like forested wetlands, most nonforested wetlands occur in the floodplains of rivers and streams, upland depressions or sinkholes, and seeps or springs.

A **marsh** is a wetland that is dominated by herbaceous plants, especially members of the sedge family, such as sedges, rushes, and bulrushes, as well as other wetland plants such as cattail, rose-mallow, bur-reed, beak-rushes, and smartweeds. Marsh communities are usually flooded in winter and spring,

A wet meadow in Laurel County that contains more than half a dozen state-listed plant species..

A marsh with state threatened southern wild rice.

Pinkster-flowered azalea in an acid seep, an important wetland community for several rare plants.

Cobble bars along rivers in southeastern Kentucky sometimes have an unusual flora, including prairie plants and numerous rare species.

and the soil usually remains saturated the rest of the year, except during droughts. **Wet meadows** tend to be drier in the late summer and fall than a marsh and have more grasses and wildflowers and fewer sedges and rushes. Natural wet meadows are very rare. Most developed after disturbance; therefore, they are called seminatural communities.

An unusual and rare type of wetland is the **seep**. Seeps occur where water percolates (seeps) out of the earth, often at the base of a hill or slope, but sometimes up on the slope. These seeps can be forested or nonforested. They often are carpeted with sphagnum and other mosses, which in turn support an assemblage of ferns and wildflowers that are adapted to growing in the saturated substrate. Cinnamon fern and royal fern are two characteristic plants of this habitat, as are cardinal-flower, turtlehead, smooth phlox, and arrow-leaved tearthumb.

Another kind of wetland is the riverine **gravel/cobble bar,** which occurs in our streams and rivers. Usually these gravel bars support a variety of weedy native and nonnative plants that can withstand drought during the summer as well as periodic flooding and high-velocity water during the winter and spring. Composition of this habitat varies from site to site, but typical plants include smartweeds, water-willow, and ragweed.

There is a unique version of this community that occurs in several streams in the Cumberland Plateau of southeastern Kentucky. The bars here are well developed with boulders mixed with sand and gravel. The flora, besides comprising the typical plants of other bars, is rich in prairie and coastal plain species and other unusual plants. The open areas of the bars have grasses such as big bluestem, Indian grass, and little bluestem. Blazing-stars, obedient plants, and coneflowers add to the prairielike appearance. This is a good example of a rare community that supports rare species.

To understand the relationship of rarity to extinction and plant conservation, it is important to understand rarity itself. When is a plant considered "rare" and what are the natural causes of rarity? Interest in the rarity of plants has a long history, but the reasons for our interest vary. Rarity adds instant value to anything. Stamps, toys, coins, cars, even houses—the fewer there are, the more value they hold. The same is true for plants. In seventeenth-century Europe, a craze over tulips captivated the culture and economy. At this time tulips became one of the most valuable commodities in Europe—not just valuable plants but *the* most sought-after collectible and an investment that could make, or break, a speculating investor. Some of the rarer tulips were worth twelve times the typical salary of that day—more than the average home. Also, tulip growers had to wait seven years for a new tulip cultivar to bloom before they could determine whether it was uniquely beautiful and ultimately sellable. Fortunes were made and lost on the rarity of tulips.

Orchids have a mystique that has attracted collectors for more than 800 years, and, like tulips, the rarer the orchid, the greater the obsession. In the early 1800s wealthy Englishmen spent fortunes sending botanical explorers on collection trips to the wild unknown, usually South America, to find new orchid species. Boatloads of orchids were brought back to England, and then another fortune was spent trying to grow them. The obsession began as an appreciation for the beauty of these complex plants, but eventually orchid collection fed into a competitive lust after trophies and fame. Susan Orleans in the *The Orchid Thief* writes of an "orchidelirium" during this period: "Because orchid hunters hated the thought of another hunter's finding any plant they might have missed, they would 'collect out' an area, then they would burn the place down." Certain plant groups, orchids and trilliums in particular, naturally seem to feed the obsession to collect plants from the wild. These groups are popular among hobbyists, and, as is the case with any other hobby, there are a few collectors who become obsessive. But the reason we should care about rare plants is not simply because they are a "hot commodity"; it is because they are critical indicators of environmental health as well as important to our natural heritage.

Rarity in plant species means that there are a low number of populations. As has been discussed, a plant usually becomes rare because of habitat loss or related pressures and threats. There are also some plants that are naturally rare. Three characteristics that are used to categorize types of rarity, apart from any influence from human disturbance, are geographic range, habitat specialization, and the total number of populations. If a plant has a small range, occurs in a specialized habitat, and has few populations, it is obvious that this plant would be considered rare. But there are other combinations

Limestone fame-flower, endangered in Kentucky.

Cumberland sandwort, state and federally endangered.

of these factors that result in rarity. Here are a few examples from Kentucky.

Narrow Range, Specialized Habitat

Kentucky is not generally a land of extremes. It is a middle ground between the cold north and the tropics, and therefore the stresses on plants here are comparatively minimal, with some exceptions. Kentucky does not have the coldest or the hottest or the highest or the lowest habitat extremes. Also, it is in the middle of a big land mass, North America. The floras of states like Florida and Hawaii have been physically isolated for a long time and tend to have a high percentage of plants that are endemic and are also globally rare. There are other factors, but habitat extremes and isolation contribute to the number of rare species that are endemic in an area. It is not surprising that there are not a lot of endemics in the Kentucky flora, since it is contiguous with several regional floras.

Only two plants among the hundreds considered rare are true endemics to Kentucky: white-haired goldenrod and Kentucky glade cress. These plants, like many endemics, are associated with highly unusual habitats. Kentucky glade cress is found with a certain type of dolomitic limestone that is uncommon. White-haired goldenrod occurs in or near rockhouses, which are shallow recesses in the sides of ravines. The availability of habitat is most likely limiting the distribution of these plants.

A few other species have a very narrow range but occur in two different states, usually near the state borders. These are called near-endemics. Three of these are limestone fame-

Short's goldenrod, a near-endemic that is state and federally endangered.

flower, Cumberland sandwort, and Short's goldenrod. Two of these have stories similar to those of Kentucky endemics. Fame-flower is a species occurring in open limestone glades, and it is limited generally to the Nashville, Tennessee, area (physiographically, the Nashville Basin) and a few occurrences around Bowling Green, Kentucky. Cumberland sandwort is restricted to rockhouses along the Kentucky-Tennessee border. Short's goldenrod has a history associated with bison migration and was, until a recent discovery of a population in Indiana, known to occur only in Kentucky.

Wide Range, Specialized Habitat

One of the most confusing forms of rarity is that of plants with a wide range but which are rare throughout that range. The wide range seems to imply that they might at one time have been more common, but that is not always the case. This kind of distribution is typical of species that are found in seeps. Acid seeps, wet openings that result from an extrusion of groundwater at the land surface, are small, isolated wetland systems surrounded by trees. These little gems of biodiversity often support rare plant species. Some species in acid seeps were never common simply because seeps are so uncommon. For example, the populations of white fringeless orchid in Kentucky, a species that is a candidate for federal listing as endangered or threatened, are congregated in southeastern Kentucky, but many of these are widely separated from one another by miles of unsuitable habitat. The topography where seeps form is relatively flat, with low, rolling undulations. These low, flat areas are also preferred for development and agriculture, which further jeopardizes the fragile seep habitats and, as they disappear, increases the distance between orchid populations. What is the likelihood that a species will survive with its populations separated by miles of prime residential land?

Wide Range, Habitat Frequent

An even more puzzling kind of rarity is that of a plant whose populations are widespread and whose habitat is not particularly uncommon. This seems to be the case for heart-leaved plantain. It is distributed widely throughout the eastern United States and into Canada, yet it is rare in all 18 states where it is or was known. It has not been seen in Kentucky since around 1869. Though the habitat, gravelly areas along streams, is somewhat specialized, this habitat commonly occurred along perennial streams in Kentucky. Researchers believe that production of a large fleshy plant reduces resources available for reproductive output (it produces very few flowers and seeds), and this characteristic, combined with poor seed dispersal, explains why this species has probably always been rare, although rampant changes to stream systems also contributed to its demise. It is now missing from five states and highly imperiled in nine states and Canada.

Factors Influencing Rarity

Plant distributions and abundance are influenced by natural factors so numerous that a complete list would be very long. This list would include widely different influences, from climate and wind currents to biological relationships (animal dispersers and pollinators) and diseases or pathogens. Geology, which affects topography, soil, and even microclimate, has already been noted as an influence on patterns of plant distribution. Unusual niches and unique conditions are created by geologic events that in turn affect plant speciation.

Genetics also accounts for some rarity in plants. As populations become smaller and more isolated, the genetic diversity of the species may decline. The more robust a plant is genetically, the more likely it will withstand stress, whether natural or manmade.

It is true, as the botanists Kruckeberg and Rabinowitz (1985) state, that "organisms do not occur where they cannot, but often they do not occur where they might." When botanists are looking for new populations of a rare plant, the fact that plants "do not occur where they might" can be confounding. Weeks may be spent surveying suitable habitat without finding a targeted plant. Some plants are just not widespread. The reasons that a plant does not occur somewhere, apart from having been eliminated by disturbance, could be that it just has not gotten there yet—it is a species that is young and still expanding. Another possibility is that it was not successful at that site or that the subtleties of suitable habitat for that particular species are not known. Something may be ecologically missing. White-haired goldenrod, for example, has not inhabited rockhouses in the southern cliff section of the Cumberland Plateau or in New River Gorge in West Virginia. This may be because there is a physical disjunction that serves as a dispersal barrier to this goldenrod and limits its expansion. Again, most plants are rare because their habitat has been lost, but there are some questions about distribution that are hard to answer even when we consider the pervasive loss of natural habitat.

Relicts

Historically, major changes in North American climate have been influenced most by glaciers, and, as glaciers altered the climate, plant distributions were tremendously changed. Kentucky's climate became much colder during the most recent Ice Age, although the glaciers only nipped the northern tip of the

state. As the glaciers receded, the warming climate became less hospitable for plants preferring colder weather, and some were extirpated. It is believed that a few of these species occurred in a microenvironment that could sustain their cold-hardy habits. These plants are called paleoendemics, species that persist in an area as relicts of a former climatic period. Mountain maple is found at the entrances to caves, where the cool air flowing from within the caves tempers the heat of the Kentucky summer. This maple of northern climates may be persisting in Kentucky as a relict of glacial history.

Peripheral Rarity

The majority of the plants considered rare in Kentucky are species that are at the edge of their natural range. Kentucky is a meeting ground for many different regional floras—Gulf Coastal Plain flora from the south, Appalachian flora influences in the east, Great Plains flora in the west, and species associated with northern temperate areas. A plant may be common in the southeastern United States, in the Gulf Coastal Plain, for instance, and barely reach this state at the northern edge of its range. For any species, life at the edge of its natural range comes with a lot of pressure. These peripheral populations must adapt to environmental situations that are more

Small white lady's-slipper, a state endangered species that grows in a unique grassland habitat.

extreme than the rest of their home range. It may be colder, for instance, than in the south. For this reason, the genetic makeup of these peripheral populations is often more diverse than that of those populations in the center of the plant's distribution. They have more tools in their tool chest to respond to environmental change.

Small white lady's-slipper, for instance, occurs in open wetlands in the northern and midwestern states (Minnesota, Nebraska, North Dakota, and then east to New Jersey). But in the southern part of its range, such as here in Kentucky, it occurs in the driest type of habitat in the region, limestone glades. This difference from one extreme habitat to the other is no doubt manifested in the genotypes, the different genetic makeup, of these populations—despite being the same species. The overall adaptability of this orchid may have been expanded as it adapted to the southern habitats. There is evidence that the world is becoming warmer, so small white lady's-slipper may need the southern genotype to survive long-term climate changes.

This leads to a legitimate question, "Why should we protect species that are common somewhere else?" It is because new species may arise from plants that occur at the edge of a species range; the edge of the range is the hotbed of adaptation to changes in the environment, and it is inevitable that change occurs. Genotypic diversity, the amount of variation in the genes of a species, is critical to a species' ability to respond to environmental pressures such as drought or disease. This ability to adapt to a changing environment is in turn critical to the stability of the flora as a whole. And the stability of the flora is the foundation of healthy ecosystems.

Extinction and the Preservation of Species

David Quammen, a renowned natural history author, states in *The Song of the Dodo: Island Biogeography in an Age of Extinctions:* "To be rare is to have a lower threshold of collective catastrophe. Any misfortune, even one that would seem small by an absolute standard, is liable to be a total misfortune. A modest-sized disaster can push a rare species immodestly close to oblivion. At the end, the last individual's death might turn out to be accidental, independent of the factors that shoved the species into the foyer of extinction." Extinction is a process, a series of events that degrade a species' ability to withstand the vicissitudes of nature. As Quammen explains, even moderately stressing events can become devastating to a plant whose numbers have been dwindling from habitat loss or competition from exotic species. It is a numbers game. The more individuals or populations of a species, the better the chance it has to withstand stressful events such as a 50-year drought or a chemical spill. But in combination with other events that have weakened the species, the drought or the chemical pollution may be its final undoing.

At some point, even if there are living individuals, the species is beyond recovery because there are too few individuals to maintain a healthy gene pool. So even though it would be tragic to lose the last group of plants, perhaps to highway construction or development, the species may have already been lost by all the preceding cumulative deaths of populations over many years. The biological tragedy occurred years before, and the last extinction is more poetic than important to the species' survivability. As we discussed, some species are naturally rare, and the more narrow the geographic distribution, the more vulnerable these species are to extinction. But many common species in Kentucky have become rare as their habitats have been degraded and eliminated. These species are just as vulnerable as those that were always rare.

Six plants have been extirpated from Kentucky, or become state-extinct. One species, stipuled scurfpea, known only from the Ohio River system, is extinct worldwide. It was last collected around 1853 and has never been seen since, perhaps because of changes in the riverbanks and hydrology. Before becoming extinct, a plant that is thought to be gone from the state is termed "historic" until more intensive surveys confirm that there is no known existing site for it in Kentucky. Showy lady's-slipper was once reported from the Corbin area and has not been found since 1888. This species is listed as historic and will soon be considered extinct in the state. A plant's first step toward extinction is to be designated as being of special concern; then, as the plant species continues to decline, it becomes threatened, endangered, historic, and, finally, extinct.

Showy lady's-slipper, a historic species in Kentucky.

The number of populations recorded for southern crabapple warranted its removal from the state list.

Conservation

Conservation of rare plants is about protecting native habitat. The stability and diversity of the native flora are fundamental to maintaining healthy ecosystems. The protection of individual species is the first step in ensuring that ecosystems remain intact and functioning. Every plant has a role in the ecosystem, and conservation efforts are aimed not only at preserving the plant itself but also at maintaining its contribution to natural systems in Kentucky.

Protection

The Rare Plant Recognition Act was enacted in 1994 to establish a list of Kentucky rare plants. Of the more than 2,000 plants in the state reported by Ronald L. Jones in his 2005 book, *Plant Life of Kentucky,* 273 are identified as endangered or threatened. The Kentucky State Nature Preserves Commission, with the help of other biologists in the conservation community, reviews information on range, abundance, and life history to identify plants that are vulnerable to decline and extinction. KSNPC administers the official list (updated every four years) as well as an annually revised list that includes plants of special concern (See Rare and Extirpated Plants of Kentucky in this volume).

The natural heritage methodology used by KSNPC to organize conservation information on species, communities, and sites was established more than 30 years ago and is used in all 50 states and internationally as well. Locations of plants, animals, and natural communities are mapped in a comprehensive system of data management, and congregations of rare plants, animals, and communities are evaluated as potential conservation targets. In this way the maximum number of species and healthy natural communities can be protected.

There are only so many people and so many dollars devoted to conservation. The organized species and site information is used to focus conservation efforts employing these limited resources. This is the reality of the business of conservation.

The U.S. Endangered Species Act provides guidance and some protection for, at present, eight plants in Kentucky. The process for listing is very rigorous, and the protection afforded by this legislation is applicable only where federal lands or funding is involved. Animals listed under the federal process are protected wherever they occur, but plants are considered the property of the landowner and are not protected on private lands unless there is some connection to federal funding. Eggert's sunflower was federally listed in 1997, and it was the first to be delisted, eight years later. This sunflower was found to be more abundant in Tennessee, and therefore it no longer

Eggert's sunflower, a state-listed species, was removed from the federal list because it was found to be more abundant in Tennessee.

New species of plants are still being discovered in Kentucky, such as swollen bladderwort, which was added as a candidate for state listing.

Cumberland sandwort
Cumberland rosemary
Running buffalo clover
Virginia spiraea
Price's potato bean
Braun's rock-cress
Short's goldenrod
White-haired goldenrod

met the criteria for federal listing. It is still considered threatened in Kentucky, however.

Rare plant habitats may be protected by establishing nature preserves and conservation easements, and there are other programs focused on landowner education and assistance. Many of these sites must also be properly and continuously managed to ensure protection. Although these tools all have their place in the recovery of rare plants, there are simply not enough conservation programs to bring about the protection of endangered species without the cooperation and ingenuity of the public.

Relocation and Growing of Rare Plants

When a rare plant is in the way of development, it is natural to wonder why we can't move it to a protected place. As undeveloped land becomes scarcer and our native flora disappears, these conflicts will become more and more common. Why won't relocating rare plants in these situations work? It may seem like a good idea to collect seed of a rare species, grow it, and spread it into new environments, but there are sound scientific reasons that do not support this method. Here are some reasons to consider.

Plants adapt to the local geography. As a plant adapts, it may develop a local genotype, or a set of genes that enable it to maximize its ability to be successful in specific ecological conditions. Because of this genotypic development, a plant from one part of a species' range may have less chance of survival in another part or could even undermine the population as a whole. Also, relocation can be risky since moved plants may eventually fail after a few years or they may have unforeseen results. Neither is wholesale growing of rare plants for distribution in the landscape a sound approach. On the other hand, new genes introduced into a population could bolster a plant's ability to adapt to new situations. A science-based plan for rare plant recovery may utilize relocation in combination with other strategies. The best conservation outcome, however, is protection of endangered plants where they naturally occur, and the larger the natural system protected, the better. In plant conservation, the whole ecosystem is worth more than the sum of its parts.

What You Can Do

Green living. Green living refers to the practice of reducing one's impact on the planet. This is becoming easier as new products, information, and resources are available to guide conservation efforts in the use of cars, managing businesses and homes, and other aspects of daily living. The availability of local products that generally reduce environmental costs of food production is increasing. Conservation of energy, water, air, and land reduces the human effects on the environment. There are positive signs that green living is becoming not only possible for moderate-income people but also a viable option on a large scale.

Support conservation organizations. Conservation organizations are a good way to pool resources and focus action. Research the goals of the various organizations and read about the issues toward which they direct their resources to determine whether they are effective. To support rare plant conservation, with contributions of either money or volunteer time, look for organizations that:

1. support laws that protect natural areas with rare plants and restrict wild collection, such as the U.S. Endangered Species Act, Kentucky's Rare Plant Recognition Act, or other, similar laws;
2. purchase or protect natural areas, especially rare plant sites;
3. manage and distribute information on rare plants or that support genetic resources for rare plant conservation.

Finally, and perhaps most important, appreciating the marvels of nature that Kentucky has to offer and sharing this experience with others provides lasting support for plant conservation. We save or protect only what we know and love, and for citizens of Kentucky, with its wonderful variety of life, there is much to protect.

The Rare Plants

The flora of the broad-leaved upland or mesophytic forests is the most familiar of Kentucky's natural lands. The spring woodland flowers—trillium, bluebell, wood poppy, bloodroot, Indian cucumber, and spring beauty—signal a renewal of life after a frozen winter. A walk in the spring woodlands is as important a ritual to many Kentuckians as Christmas tree decorating and Fourth of July picnics. Most of the spring woodland species take advantage of the coincidence of warming temperatures and leafless trees that allow increased light on the forest floor. There is a flush of flowering before the shade develops under the tree canopy. These forests are the most familiar, but there is a lot of variety in forest types in Kentucky, and forests in general are the most extensive habitat in the state. They are also home to many rare plants.

Forested communities with the rarest plants are those that, not surprisingly, are also rare themselves. For example, Cumberland highlands forest occurs exclusively at the highest elevations in the state, or essentially on Black Mountain. Remarkably, there are 30 rare plant species in this mountain ecosystem, many that are Appalachian species, and five occur nowhere else in the state.

A community unique to Pine Mountain is the Cumberland Pine Barrens, and one of the rare plants of this high and dry community occurs nowhere else in the state. Canada frostweed is a tiny plant with a flower so disproportionately large

The Cumberland highlands forest is rich and moist and has outstanding wildflower displays in the spring. Thousands of trillium can carpet the forest slopes, as they do here on Black Mountain.

Canada frostweed, a state endangered pine barrens species.

Agrimonia gryposepala	tall hairy groovebur
Angelica triquinata	filmy angelica
Anomodon rugelii	a moss
*Botrychium oneidense**	blunt-lobe grape fern
Carex aestivalis	summer sedge
Carex leptonervia	finely-nerved sedge
Carex roanensis	Roan Mountain sedge
Chrysosplenium americanum	American golden-saxifrage
Cymophyllus fraserianus	Fraser's sedge
Dryopteris carthusiana	spinulose wood fern
Eupatorium maculatum	spotted joe-pye weed
Eupatorium steelei	Steele's joe-pye weed
*Heracleum lanatum**	cow-parsnip
Hydrophyllum virginianum	eastern waterleaf
Lilium superbum	Turk's cap lily
Maianthemum canadense	wild lily-of-the-valley
Platanthera psycodes	small purple-fringed orchid
Rubus canadensis	smooth blackberry
Sambucus racemosa ssp. *pubens*	red elderberry
Saxifraga micranthidifolia	lettuce-leaf saxifrage
Silene ovata	ovate catchfly
Solidago curtisii	Curtis' goldenrod
Solidago puberula	downy goldenrod
Solidago roanensis	Roan Mountain goldenrod
Streptopus lanceolatus	rosy twisted stalk
Trillium undulatum	painted trillium
Vaccinium erythrocarpum	southern mountain cranberry
Veratrum parviflorum	Appalachian bunchflower
Viburnum lantanoides	alder-leaved viburnum

* historic

it looks as if it will topple the plant. The pines and grasses that dominate this xeric community depend on fire to persist, as do some of the rare plants, such as yellow wild indigo. Wherever this legume is found throughout the eastern United States and Canada, it is adapted to xeric, fire-mediated conditions. It has been used as a substitute, albeit a poor one, for indigo dye, and the scientific name for yellow wild indigo is *Baptisia tinctoria*; the word *baptisia* comes from the Greek for dye; the word *tinctoria* comes from the Latin for dye.

Another hotspot for rare plants is Bad Branch, the largest and deepest gorge on Pine Mountain. E. Lucy Braun, the first ecologist to provide a comprehensive description of these nat-

Vascular Plants

Baptisia tinctoria	yellow wild indigo
Botrychium matricariifolium	matricary grape fern
Boykinia aconitifolia	brook saxifrage
Circaea alpina	small enchanter's nightshade
Corydalis sempervirens	rock harlequin
Cymophyllus fraserianus	Fraser's sedge
Eupatorium steelei	Steele's joe-pye weed
Gentiana decora	showy gentian
Hexastylis contracta	southern heartleaf
Hexastylis heterophylla	variable-leaved heartleaf
Houstonia serpyllifolia	Michaux's bluet
Juglans cinerea	white walnut
Leucothoe recurva	red-twig doghobble
Listera smallii	kidney-leaf twayblade
Oenothera perennis	small sundrop
Pogonia ophioglossoides	rose pogonia
Sanguisorba canadensis	Canada burnet
Saxifraga michauxii	Michaux's saxifrage
Trillium undulatum	painted trillium

Mosses

Anomodon rugelii	
Brachythecium populeum	matted feather moss
Cirriphyllum piliferum	
Dicranodontium asperulum	
Entodon brevisetus	
Neckera pennata	
Oncophorus raui	
Polytrichum pallidisetum	a hair cap moss
Polytrichum strictum	
Sphagnum quinquefarium	a sphagnum moss

Yellow wild indigo, state threatened, is a fire-adapted species.

ural community types, recognized the significance of this area as unique in its position on the "dip," or southeastern slope, of the mountain. This rich ravine system has an enormous diversity of habitats, including spray cliffs and a permanently running stream. There are 19 rare vascular plants at Bad Branch, and as if to add an exclamation mark to this lavish diversity, 10 rare mosses are recorded here as well.

In addition to those plants that are restricted by the habitat availability of certain forest types, there are also those at

The high-elevation forest, narrow gorge, and cliffs at Bad Branch Falls, Letcher County, make this a hot spot for rare plants.

Smooth blackberry, a state endangered species, is known from only one location.

Small enchanter's nightshade, a species of special concern.

Northern starflower is a state endangered northern species that reaches its southern range in Kentucky.

the edge of their range. Small enchanter's nightshade, smooth blackberry, and northern starflower are near the southern edge of their range in Kentucky and are common species in the hardwood forests of northern temperate climates. With species names like "alpina," "canadensis," and "borealis," this is probably not a revelation. They reach this area through the Appalachian Mountains and are limited to the mountains and high hills of eastern Kentucky. Smooth blackberry is a very

Fraser's sedge, state endangered.

Painted trillium, a state threatened species, usually occurs at elevations above 3,000 feet.

distinctive species; it has a single large flower rather than the clusters of white flowers found on common blackberries.

Mountain maple, as mentioned earlier, is thought to be a relict of another age, a species left over from the flora that became established during the last glacial period. It has the unmistakable maple-shaped leaf, but in Kentucky this tree remains low growing. Braun (1950) identified other possible glacial relicts, including cotton-grass, mountain-lover, and Canada yew.

Another rare plant of forests with affinities to the Appalachian region is Fraser's sedge, a species that occurs in a few places in extreme southeastern Kentucky. It is generally harder to get people excited about protecting sedges because they're inconspicuous and all look alike. Fraser's sedge, however, is the poster pinup of sedges—its shiny, strap-shaped leaves and stalks of white thimbles of condensed flowers make it a stun-

ner. It occurs in the lushest mountain forests that have atmospheres like those of rain forests.

Painted trillium is another Appalachian species reaching southeastern Kentucky. Trilliums are distributed mostly by ants and have a special food structure on the seed that the ants collect to eat. The seeds are eventually put into an ant "trash pile" that is rich with nutrients that are perfect for nourishing these seeds. Trilliums in general are thought to have "taken refuge" from the most recent glaciers in southern regions, perhaps in the Appalachians, and then redispersed. Deer or other mammals may help with long-distance seed dispersal of painted trillium, since ant dispersal can hardly account for its wide range from Georgia to Canada.

Even among the restricted Appalachian species, southern heartleaf is unique in that it is disjunct between the Cumberland Plateaus and southeastern Blue Ridge region. Like those of wild ginger, which is closely related, the flowers lie under the leaf litter and give off a scent to attract flies and thrips, their primary pollinators.

Appalachian bugbane has a disjunct range between the Appalachian region and the Interior Low Plateaus. Instead of producing flowers that have a nectar reward for pollinators (bumblebees and larger flies), bugbane invests in producing lots of pollen. Although insects will go to bugbane, they prefer plants with nectar, and bugbane needs these plants to attract pollinators. As logging and other disturbances fragment forests, nectar plants decline, and so does bugbane. Eventually, groups of plants become isolated, and long-range pollination becomes more difficult, especially for bugbane, because at most only 20 percent of a population usually flowers. It is rare in five of the seven states in which it occurs.

Some forest wildflowers are infamous as well as endangered, and blue monkshood, an Appalachian species of mesic forests, is among them because it is poisonous. This species has been used as an anesthetic and can numb skin even on casual contact. The potential for a poisonous dose was once so worrisome that apparently early herbalists thought it was not worth the risk and rarely used this plant. Other rare forest plants have poisonous parts, including filmy angelica (poisonous flowers), fly-poison (bulbs and leaves that can cause respiratory failure), and eastern sweetshrub (poisonous seeds).

(above) Southern heartleaf, state endangered.

(left) Appalachian bugbane, state threatened.

Filmy angelica, state endangered, is a high-elevation northern species.

Fly-poison, a state threatened species that is highly toxic, especially its bulbs.

Blue monkshood, state threatened, occurs near streams in rich woods in eastern Kentucky.

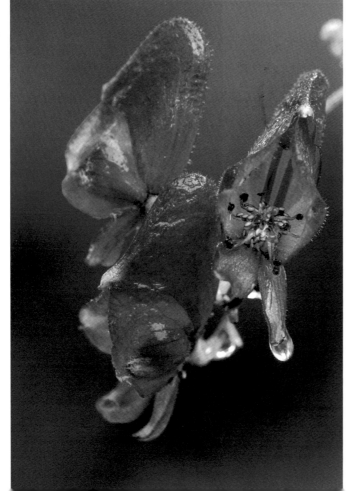

Conjurer's nut, a shrub of dry ridgetop forests that also goes by the name of leechbush, is known from a single site in Kentucky, although it is possibly overlooked elsewhere. Like the two rare false foxgloves, it is a hemiparasite, meaning it can parasitize other plants for nutrients but also has chlorophyll and so produces its own food. Conjurer's nut is dioecious: it has male and female flowers on different plants. This characteristic can add to a plant's susceptibility to habitat fragmentation.

Rare plant occurrences in the forests of central and western Kentucky are scattered; there are not many hotspots or concentrations of them. The Kentucky River watershed in the Bluegrass region, however, has an exceptional number. A combination of the cliffs of the Kentucky River, called the Pali-

The geologic features of the Kentucky River Palisades not only are spectacular, but they also support a rich diversity of rare plants.

Globe bladderpod, state endangered, grows along limestone cliffs.

Running buffalo clover, state threatened and federally endangered, is known from the Bluegrass region.

sades, and the geologic history of this part of the Inner Bluegrass region created unique conditions for the development of plant species. A group of rare plants associated with the Kentucky River drainage in the Inner Bluegrass region has disjunct occurrences around Nashville, Tennessee. These two areas have similar Ordovician Age bedrock, and presumably the geologic history of this type of bedrock has influenced the distribution of these plants. Braun's rock-cress is a spring wildflower in these forests; it has small, subtle pink flowers on a plant with gray-green foliage. The most impressive characteristic of the species is the small, star-shaped hairs that cover the lower leaf and dull the green color. It occurs in places where the soil is bare, such as limestone ledges, the downslope sides of trees, and turkey scratching sites. Braun's rock-cress is one of only eight federally listed plants in the state. Its range is limited to three Kentucky counties, Franklin, Owen, and Henry. A few populations have been found in Tennessee, but Kentucky is almost entirely responsible for the continued existence of this endangered plant.

Globe bladderpod is a biennial associated with dry limestone outcroppings. This is one of the rarest species in Kentucky and, to date, there have been very limited opportunities to protect it. Population sizes fluctuate wildly from year to year: one year abundant, and the next nearly disappeared.

Some rare plants are not characteristic of any one natural community; one of these is running buffalo clover. Today it is most commonly found on forested stream terraces in the Bluegrass region, probably because so much of this region's natural forests have been cleared and altered. It is also occasionally found in upland mesic forests or even lawns; West Virginia populations are in oak-hickory forests. This species needs disturbance such as stream scour, animal trails (perhaps bison

traces in the past), or other small-scale disturbances. It was collected in the Lexington area in 1834, and there is speculation that a clover described in pioneer accounts may be this same species. Dreamy visions of men on horseback looking over a landscape of big trees and acres of clover among the buffalo trails are conjured in our minds by these early settlers' descriptions. The enigmatic nature of this species has also confounded attempts to come up with a conservation strategy. Running buffalo clover needs disturbance—but not too much. Can disturbance be used as management tool in these days of aggressive pest plants without constant manicuring of the forest groundcover? Would people get used to bison in

(clockwise from left) Tennessee leafcup, small-flower baby-blue-eyes, and blue scorpion-weed are, respectively, state endangered, threatened, and of special concern; all occur in western Kentucky.

Price's potato bean is a state endangered and federally threatened species that occurs in western Kentucky.

their backyards? Of course, that's not an option, but running buffalo clover continues to decline as we attempt to piece together a method to recover this species.

In the forests of far western Kentucky, the East Gulf Coastal Plains, and the Mississippi Alluvial Plain, several plants adapted to the wind-deposited silty soil, or loess, on the river bluffs are rare. Small-flower baby-blue-eyes, blue scorpion-weed, and Tennessee leafcup are found in these ravines.

An especially rare plant in this western region is Price's potato bean, or groundnut. It is federally listed as threatened and occurs from Mississippi to Kentucky. It once grew as far north as Illinois, but now Kentucky is the northernmost extent of its range. Whether this species was much more common at one time or whether it has always been rare is not clear. Native Americans and pioneers used a related and similar-looking groundnut as a food plant, and, because this rare vine forms a large underground tuber, it seems very possible that it was collected for food as well. Collection could have rapidly depleted this plant because it takes years to establish a substantial-size tuber. Price's potato bean is found on open, rocky, steep slopes along streams and clearly needs sunshine to produce flowers.

The rare plants in the following photos are from a variety of forest communities from the high elevation forest to the bluffs of the Mississippi River.

Rosy twisted stalk 🌿 The flowers of rosy twisted stalk hang from the subtle kinks in the stem like bells. The plant may be mistaken for Solomon's seal, a cousin in the lily family complex. Its red berries are eaten by birds.

Turk's cap lily 🌿 The reflexed petals of this tall, striking lily help to distinguish it from other species.

Appalachian bunchflower 🌿 Bunchflower, a member of the lily family, may appear as inconspicuous leaves for years and then produce a six-foot-tall stalk of flowers.

Red elderberry 🍂 Not only does this species differ from common elderberry by having bright red berries, but it also has a conical rather than flat-topped arrangement of flowers.

Steele's joe-pye weed 🦋 Steele's joe-pye weed is a southern Appalachian endemic and has glandular-pubescent leaves and stems, which make it easy to identify. Like most members of this genus of plants, it is an excellent butterfly nectar plant.

Allegheny-vine Allegheny-vine looks like a vining fern; it scrambles in rich, moist, shady sites at upper elevations. Other common names are climbing bleeding heart (a related genus) and mountain fringe.

Eastern waterleaf There are four species of waterleaf in Kentucky; this eastern species has three to seven leaf divisions. It is also known as Indian salad because the young leaves can be eaten like lettuce.

Roan Mountain goldenrod 🍃 Roan Mountain goldenrod is associated with the northern hardwoods on Black Mountain.

Curtis' goldenrod 🍃 The grooves in the stem of Curtis' goldenrod, generally a high elevation species, help to distinguish it from other goldenrod species.

American lily-of-the-valley 🍃 The European species is familiar to many gardeners as a prolific and sometimes weedy plant, but the American lily-of-the-valley does not have that reputation. The spring-blooming flowers have the same wonderful scent.

Wild lily-of-the-valley 🍃 The wild lily-of-the-valley is named after the European lily-of-the-valley because the leaves look similar, but it is not as strongly rhizomatous. It is found in mountainous areas in Kentucky.

Showy gentian   Showy gentian, despite the name, is the smallest of the gentians occurring in Kentucky, although it is just as lovely as any other.

Common silverbell 🍃 This understory tree has been cultivated because of its showy spring flowers.

Michaux's bluet 🌼 Michaux's bluet, a high-elevation species, is different from the common bluet in having a stem that is prostrate rather than erect, and the inside of the flower is hairy.

Small purple-fringed orchid 🌼 The two purple-fringed orchids (*Platanthera grandiflora* and Kentucky's *P. psycodes*) are reproductively isolated by the size of their flowers. The Kentucky species is the smaller and attracts moths (by night) and butterflies (by day) with shorter tongues, or proboscises.

Lettuce-leaf saxifrage Lettuce-leaf saxifrage occurs on wet rocks within the rushing waters of mountain streams. It has traditionally been used as salad greens.

Canada burnet Canada burnet is a northern temperate species that barely reaches Kentucky; in fact, it is found in only one place in Kentucky.

Kidney-leaf twayblade 🌿 This little orchid, in fact the smallest in Kentucky, is sometimes found beneath rhododendron thickets.

Matricary grape fern 🌿 Matricary grape fern produces a single small leaf each year (common grape fern has three). It is found in a single county in Kentucky.

Michaux's saxifrage 🌸 The yellow-spotted flower petals of Michaux's saxifrage are distinctive for this species. It is found in rich woods and on wet, rocky ledges.

Red buckeye 🌸 Red buckeye is a shrub or small tree occurring in far western Kentucky. It is an excellent source of nectar for hummingbirds.

Blue jasmine leatherflower   The bell-shaped flowers of this clematis are sometimes two-toned, blue or lavender and white. It is associated with Mississippi River floodplain swamps.

Snow squarestem 🌸 Snow squarestem is at the northern edge of its Coastal Plain range in Kentucky. It is found in shady woods near swamps.

Spotted mandarin 🌸 Spotted mandarin is similar to the more common mandarin, but its purple-spotted flowers and red berries make it is easy to distinguish.

Small yellow lady's-slipper 🌸 Though flies and other small insects may visit the flowers of small yellow lady's-slipper, it is probably bees that are most successful in pollinating this diminutive orchid.

Beaked yellow trout lily This group of lilies gets its name from its bloom time: when the trout begin to run. This northern species dips into the northeastern part of the state and has petals that are very reflexed, or bent back.

Appalachian rosinweed Appalachian rosinweed is found in forests with high light conditions and increases after fire and limited tree removal.

Allegheny chinkapin 🌿 Allegheny chinkapin is a low-growing shrub of dry, rocky forests in eastern Kentucky.

Sweet pinesap 🌿 The sweet scent produced by this plant often can be smelled before the plant is seen, especially since it is the color of leaf litter.

Gaywings  The flower of gaywings looks like a little pink airplane, low to the ground.

Mock-orange 🌿 The flowers of this species of mock-orange are scentless, unusual in a genus known for its fragrant flowers.

Hoary mock-orange  The undersides of the hoary mock-orange's leaves are fuzzy, and, unlike the other rare mock-orange, its flowers are fragrant. Mock-orange is commonly used as a food or nectar plant by moths and butterflies.

Green-and-gold 🌿 Green-and-gold is a low-growing groundcover found in southeastern Kentucky.

Buckley's goldenrod 🌿 Buckley's goldenrod is a midwestern species, thus found only in western Kentucky, the eastern edge of its range. Its habitat is dry forests.

Lesser rattlesnake-plantain 🌿 This species is similar to the common rattlesnake-plantain, but the leaves have a more mottled pattern. It is found in one cool, moist forest in Kentucky. Like other orchids, it requires that a specific fungus to be present in the soil for it to become established.

Whorled horse-balm 🌿 This mint of the southern Appalachians is rare throughout its range. It is related to the more northern horse-balm but differs in having fewer leaves that are not widely scattered on the stem.

Least trillium The taxonomy and distribution of least trillium are not fully understood. There are probably two different varieties in Kentucky, one occurring in swamps and one found in calcareous forest.

Snow trillium  Snow trillium blooms so early in the spring that it is occasionally blanketed with snow.

Wood lily 🍃 Wood lily is associated with woodlands with grassy under-stories and openings in the canopy. Unfortunately, with the decline in this habitat, this plant now occurs along roads at the edges of forests.

Spotted coral-root 🍃 Two of the coral-roots in the state are separated by bloom time; this rare species is the summer-blooming spotted coral-root.

Carolina anglepod Carolina anglepod is a vine in the milkweed family.

White walnut 🍂 White walnut, or butternut, is threatened throughout its range by an introduced fungus. It is rare to find a healthy tree of this once-common species.

Appalachian sedge　Appalachian sedge, a species of dry forests in eastern Kentucky, is at the western edge of its range in this state.

Star tickseed　Most of the occurrences of star tickseed are in sandy alluvial woods in the Big South Fork area.

Wood's bunchflower   Wood's bunchflower is found low on limestone slopes. The strap-shaped leaves have parallel venation (that is, the leaf veins are parallel), and they are large for a perennial herb, which makes them easily noticed on the forest floor.

Buffalo clover Buffalo clover, like the other rare clover, running buffalo clover, responds to disturbance, but it is found in drier habitats in the western part of the state.

Softleaf arrowwood This viburnum is found on wooded slopes in
limestone regions of Kentucky, primarily the Palisades.

Ovate catchfly 🍃 Though widely scattered throughout the southeastern United States and northward to Indiana and Illinois, ovate catchfly is considered rare throughout its range.

Mercury spurge 🌿 Mercury spurge is at its northern range limit in Kentucky. It has a milky sap, or latex, that is high in alkaloids and can be toxic.

Northern white cedar 🍃 Northern white cedar is found in isolated clumps associated with cave openings along streams and on cliff edges in Kentucky.

American cow-wheat 🍃 Both cow-wheat varieties, members of the snapdragon family, are rare in the state.

Rock skullcap  Rock skullcap is a mint of rocky forests in eastern Kentucky.

Grasslands and particularly glade communities are generally very hot and very dry; they may even be very wet, then dry. Species that can survive in this environment have adaptations that are similar to those of desert species: they have to be able to use and store water efficiently. Plants with long and large taproots, which take years of underground development before an aboveground plant is produced, are typical in glades and prairies. Other plants have adapted by reducing the number or size of leaves or, like cacti, by increasing their ability to store water. The native false aloe is a common glade plant and a classic xerophyte, or a plant adapted to low-water conditions. It has leaves with a thick, succulent structure, spines that reduce the surface area of the leaf, and a whitish or glaucous color—all adaptations that reduce the effects of the hot glade and prairie conditions. It also has a bulbous base, which conserves water.

As prairies and glades have declined, many of the plants that depend on these habitats have become rare. One of the most notable of the rare plants found in and around glade communities is Short's goldenrod. It was originally found in the mid-nineteenth century by C. W. Short, a physician with a passion for botany, at the Falls of the Ohio, where bison crossed the Ohio River. The McAlpin Dam was built on this site and the plant was never found there again. About one hundred years later, E. Lucy Braun found Short's goldenrod at Blue

Prairie June grass, state endangered.

Great Plains ladies'-tresses is a state threatened species.

Kentucky's bison at Blue Licks in the 1770s: "They reached the vicinity of May's Lick where they fell in with the great buffalo trace, which in a few hours brought them to the Great Blue Lick. The flats upon each side of the river were crowded with immense herds of buffalo, that had come down from the interior for the sake of salt" (*Happy Hunting Ground*, 1991). Because Short's goldenrod was curiously limited to this site, it is likely that this species developed in these open, trampled glade communities and the grassy ledges along the Licking River. As pastures were converted to fescue and land and river use continued to change in the Bluegrass region, the likelihood of this plant's persisting declined.

The first thing you notice on coming to a glade or prairie in spring is the orange-flowered hoary puccoon and yellow star-grass. In summer it's the purple and yellow coneflowers that draw attention and, in autumn, the sunflowers and obedient plant. In a good-quality glade, the grassy backdrop for the colorful perennials, important and unnoticed, is made up of an amazing number of different species of sedges, rushes, and grasses. These species are critically important to the development of these systems, especially those that have adapted to repeated grazing and burning. One adaptation that has contributed to the development of grasslands in general is the position of the apical meristem, the growing point of the plant; on some prairie grasses, it is at the base of the plant: when the top is bitten off or burned, the plant rebounds. Northern dropseed and June grass, two rare grasses in Kentucky, occur throughout the grasslands of the Great Plains, especially tall-grass prairies, but in the eastern United States, their grassland habitat is limited. Northern dropseed is a bunchgrass and is adapted to natural disturbances such as grazing and fire, which stimulate its growth. June grass is a cool-season grass, which means it grows in the spring and in the fall, whereas

Licks, Kentucky. This is the only place in Kentucky where it is known to exist, despite botanical searches of old bison trails and "gladey" habitat throughout the Bluegrass region. Blue Licks was renowned for its mineral licks, which attracted wildlife, including prehistoric animals and, later, bison. Accounts of this area describe the vegetation as extensively trampled by the bison that were attracted to the lick. Here is one account of the legendary frontiersman Simon Kenton's encounter with warm-season prairie grasses grow in the summer. Because June grass emerges early, while other grasses are still dormant, it may be intensely grazed; however, it will decrease under this grazing pressure. Ringseed rush and Crawe's sedge, two more rare species, are found around the edges of flat rocky outcrops where moisture persists in the spring.

Another rare plant of these open grasslands is the Great Plains ladies'-tresses. This terrestrial orchid is unusual in that it blooms in autumn, usually October. The flowers have a strong vanilla-like scent and form a long, cream-colored spiral among the grasses.

Royal catchfly is a rare plant that has a classic hummingbird-pollinated flower shaped like a long, red tube. Hummingbirds buzz around the flowers in regular flight patterns as they pollinate flower after flower. If hummingbirds are prevented from reaching the flowers, fruit production dramatically decreases, so the red color, which insects cannot see and birds can, is clearly important to the reproductive success of this species. Deer are able to spot this brilliant red as well. A farmer in Hardin County noticed that deer were eating all the royal catchfly flowers and built a fence around the population. The number of plants shot up several hundred percent, and all bloomed madly. Fire stimulates the seed to germinate as well as maintains its habitat. This is one of the most endangered plants in the state, and, in fact, there is no single population that occurs in a natural community; they are all relegated to roadsides or remnant patches of prairie in fields. Royal catchfly is associated with prairies where the soils are deep—rather than the thin soils of glades—and easy to plow. The ease of conversion of this habitat to farmland has no doubt contributed to the decline of these natural communities and this plant. It was formerly widely scattered from McCreary and Powell counties to Elizabethtown; it was probably connected with the prairie regions in Missouri, through western Kentucky. It is now known to exist only in Hart and Hardin counties.

Ear-leaf false foxglove is unusual in that it is an annual and a hemiparasite, a plant that will attach itself to other plants to take water and minerals. It is known to be parasitic on several grasses, coneflowers, and sunflowers. The leaves have distinctive lobes, or ears, at their bases. This plant was found in Kentucky only a few years ago, in 1998, at Crooked Creek Barrens State Nature Preserve, a woodland and prairie preserve near Maysville; then another population was discovered on the other side of the state, at Fort Campbell. Fort Campbell, like many military bases, has become a refuge for prairie plants and animals. The bases protect the land from development and cultivation, and the weaponry practice repeatedly burns the landscape and creates ideal conditions for prairie plants to persist.

Kentucky glade cress has the unfortunate fate of living within commuting distance of Louisville. Its fate was further sealed with the construction of additional exits along I-65 that provide easy access to Bullitt County. Ecologically, this is like a robin's nesting next to a houseful of cats—the chances of reproductive success drop considerably. The global range of this inches-high plant is southern Jefferson and northern Bullitt counties. It is associated with an unusual dolomitic limestone that has a notable amount of magnesium, which may explain why this plant is so rare. In the spring glade cress is sprinkled across these natural rocky openings. It inhabits soil that thinly covers limestone and is generally inhospitable to most other plants. These habitats can have temperatures of more than 100 degrees in the summer and be wet in the spring and dry a few weeks later. The species, an annual, takes advantage of the wet spring and blooms, disperses seed, and is long gone by summer.

Limestone fame-flower is similar to Kentucky glade cress

in that it is found exclusively around flat limestone outcrops, but this species is found west of Bowling Green. It is about the same size as glade cress—three to six inches tall. Fame-flower has a neon-pink flower that opens very predictably around three or four o'clock in the afternoon. It has succulent little leaves that are clustered at its base, and the flower sits atop a wire-thin stem. It is able to live in a little soil mixed with a lot of gravel scattered on a sheet of rock. The features of the plant, the succulent leaves and conservative flowering structure, are typical of desert species, and the glade habitat is just as xeric as a desert. Another species of fame-flower has the same story with a sandstone theme.

Carolina larkspur is limited to three counties in south-central Kentucky. Delphinums are commonly sold as garden perennials since the flowers are lovely, but all species are also extremely poisonous. Ingestion of any part of the plant can lead to nervous and respiratory failure. Carolina larkspur has

Roundleaf fame-flower, state endangered.

Carolina larkspur, state threatened.

long nectar spurs that are helpful in guiding the butterflies and moths that commonly pollinate them.

Scarlet Indian paintbrush occurs as splashes of red against the stark limestone of open glades. The source of this color, in Kentucky often appearing as a more luminous orange-red, is actually modified leaves; the flowers are a more subdued yellow. The species typically occurs in grasslands, and with good reason: it is semiparasitic on grasses.

Barrens silky aster is a silver-leaved aster and one of the eas-ier to recognize. This group of plants, the asters, is notorious for being difficult to tell apart. Like all "composites" (plants in the aster plant family), the pink flower is actually several small ray flowers (those extending away from the center head like petals) and a crowded bunch of disc flowers in the center. It blooms in the fall, as all asters do.

The plants shown in the following photographs are all rare plants found in prairies, woodlands, and glades.

Barrens silky aster, a species of special concern.

Scarlet Indian paintbrush is state endangered.

Blue wild indigo Blue wild indigo is generally a plant of glade communities and a smaller version of a related variety that is associated with rivers. The flowers are pollinated by bees, usually long-tongued species, and the leaves, though eaten by caterpillars of butterflies such as certain skippers, are poisonous, which deters browsing by mammals.

Slender blazing-star 🍂 Like all the members of the genus *Liatris,* slender blazing-star attracts butterflies. It is the only blazing-star on the Kentucky rare plant listing at present, but many of them are grassland-dependent species; as these plant communities continue to decline, other blazing-star species may be added. This species has a disjunct range in the state, occurring in northern Kentucky and In the glades around Bowling Green.

Purple prairie-clover 🍂 Purple prairie-clover is widely scattered from Arizona to Alabama to British Columbia to Ontario but limited to the Pennyroyal Plain region in Kentucky. After a burn, this typical grassland species not only resprouts from a thick woody taproot but increases in numbers and flowering. Like a lot of legumes, it "fixes" nitrogen in the soil, which makes it more available to other plants.

Hairy hawkweed Hairy hawkweed has inch-long, almost draping white hairs all over the plant, which deter grazing animals and also reduce evaporation from the leaf surface. It flowers in late summer, as do a lot of species in the aster family. The common name hawkweed comes from a myth that hawks ate this plant to improve their eyesight.

Small sundrop Small sundrops are associated with prairies and glades, but in the low, wet spots within these very dry systems.

Yellow gentian The flowers of yellow gentian vary from white to yellow and are commonly pollinated by bumblebees, which may buzz the flower to release the edible pollen.

Sweet coneflower  Sweet coneflower is not a coneflower, but one of the black-eyed Susans in the genus *Rudbeckia.* This genus was named for father and son botanists who were predecessors of Linnaeus. The species name is *subtomentosa.* (*sub* meaning "under" and *tomentosa* meaning "hairy"), which indicates that the undersides of the leaves are hairy.

Compass-plant A member of the aster family, this robust prairie species grows up to 10 feet tall, and its taproot is equally long. The compass-plant's flowers, like sunflowers, follow the sun as it travels across the sky.

Side-oats grama ▷ Side-oats grama is one of the most important warm-season range grasses of the Great Plains, but it is surprising that it is widely distributed from southern Canada through Central America to South America.

Prairie gentian ▷ Prairie gentian will decline if woody species invade its grassy habitat and shade the plants. It is adapted to periodic fire, which maintains the open character of a prairie.

Eastern silvery aster 🌿 Eastern silvery aster has silky, silvery leaves and a thick-rooted base, both adaptations to hot, dry habitats and the natural fires that shape this environment. Fire suppression has contributed to its decline.

Price's aster 🌿 Sadie Price was an extraordinary botanist of the late 1800s who resided in Bowling Green. One pastor called her a "true high priestess of nature." Five species have been named after her, including this showy rare aster.

Cream wild indigo 🌼 Cream wild indigo is a spring-blooming prairie and dry woodland species that is found in the far western part of the state. Like tumbleweeds, the plant breaks off at its base when its fruit are mature, and it is blown about to disperse the seeds.

White rattlesnake-root The genus name for white rattlesnake-root, *Prenanthes,* means "drooping blossom." The range of this species is generally north from Kentucky.

Nodding rattlesnake-root Nodding rattlesnake-root is related to lettuces, and its leaves bear some resemblance to them. The flower nectar attracts bees.

Purple rattlesnake-root 🌿 Purple rattlesnake-root was rediscovered in
Kentucky and is a candidate for state listing.

Gattinger's lobelia 🌿 Kentucky is the northern edge of the range of
Gattinger's lobelia, although there is only a single known occurrence.

Soft-hairy false gromwell There are three closely related species of false gromwells in Kentucky. They are coarse, hairy perennials, a habit no doubt intended to deter browsers.

Tansy rosinweed The seeds of tansy rosinweed are eaten by goldfinches, which perch on the tall (up to six feet) fruiting stem.

Narrow-leaved blue-curls 🌱 The stamens in the flowers of blue-curls are so very long that they curl up at their ends.

Nettle-leaf sage 🌱 Nettle-leaf sage flowers are blue with white nectar guides to attract insects. This salvia is a sun-loving plant and is threatened when woody species become established in natural openings.

Hairy snoutbean   Hairy snoutbean is declining in Kentucky, along with the xeric pine-oak woodland community. This little legume now persists in roadsides and utility rights-of-way, some of the only open grassy habitats remaining in the area.

Crawe's sedge   There are 23 species from the sedge genus *Carex* that are considered rare; across the state there are a total of 125 *Carex* species. This sedge occupies the thin-soiled edges of glades and similar habitats.

Stemless evening primrose   Occurrence of stemless evening primrose is hard to predict since this plant inhabits exposed, often gravelly ground, which may temporarily result from erosion.

Rock harlequin 🌸 Rock harlequin is found in rock crevices at upper elevations in eastern Kentucky. It is widely distributed in Canada and southward in the eastern United States in mountainous regions.

Appalachian sandwort ❧ Appalachian sandwort is an annual that flowers, fruits, and then germinates in the fall to overwinter as small plants. Its habitat is sandstone rock outcrops and cliff ledges.

Racemed milkwort ❧ Milkworts such as racemed milkwort were thought to stimulate milk production in grazing animals. This species is found in sandy openings in southeastern Kentucky.

Wedge-leaf whitlow-grass Wedge-leaf whitlow-grass is not a grass but an annual that is only three to eight inches tall and is one of the very earliest spring-flowering plants in the open glade habitats of western Kentucky.

Hispid false mallow Hispid false mallow occurs in a dry, grassy glade habitat. It was once widely distributed in central Kentucky, but as this habitat has declined, so has the number of occurrences.

Upland privet 🌿 Upland privet, a small shrub in the ash family, is associated with the perimeters of open glades in central Kentucky.

Cutleaf meadow-parsnip 🌿 Like all members of the carrot family, cutleaf meadow-parsnip has a flat-topped head of tiny flowers. The taxonomy of several closely related species is being studied to define the species clearly.

Necklace glade cress The name of this glade cress is derived from the appearance of the seeds bulging as if strung together in the pod. Habitat for this species is the edges of or small depressions among exposed rocky openings that have a hint of soil.

Ten-lobe false foxglove Ten-lobe false foxglove, one of six species in this genus in the state, is found in woodlands. Butterflies and long-tongued bees, such as bumblebees, pollinate the flowers.

Whether too much water or not enough, extreme conditions are common in rivers. One day there are torrents of rushing water ripping at roots, and before long the river appears to be a gently meandering stream or is even completely dry. These changing water levels put tremendous stress on river systems. Plants of every natural system have their own ecological burdens to bear, but the conditions that river plants endure make them some of the toughest species on the endangered plant list. So why are they declining?

Some aquatic plants of rivers actually live underwater. Thread-foot, one rare aquatic plant, anchors itself on rocks in rivers by producing a cementlike compound in its roots. It is known to occur in the Red River (the eastern one) and the Green, Rockcastle, and Big South Fork rivers. Thread-foot looks a lot like reddish algae because of its very thin, long leaves, a shape that reduces the friction (and stress) of life in a river current. The plant flowers very quickly when the water recedes and exposes it to air. Pollen is blown from one small flower (just a few millimeters wide) to the next and, within a few days of pollination, the fruit is already releasing mature seed. The seed is sticky and, with luck, finds a rock protected from the full force of the current. This process is very precarious: if the water level doesn't go down or the pollen or seed isn't successful, then thread-foot does not reproduce. Another remarkable quality of this plant is that not only is it sensitive

Goldenclub, state threatened.

Cumberland rosemary, state endangered and federally threatened, is known from only one boulder bar in Kentucky.

Barbara's-buttons, state endangered, is found on one cobble bar in the state.

to changes in river hydrology, but it also must have clean water. It is an excellent indicator of good water quality. It is in our best interest that this plant thrives.

Other plants on the river shoreline always have their roots in water but are only completely submerged during flood periods. One of these is goldenclub. It has large, elliptical blue-green and silver leaves that have Gore-tex–like surfaces that allow water to bead up and run off. The flowers are borne on an erect candlelike structure (spadix). This plant is so striking that it is vulnerable to overcollection for aquatic gardens. It is also vulnerable to changes in water levels and related stresses.

Though weedy plants commonly occur on many river bars (the natural flooding creates habitats open for colonization), high-quality streams in the Cumberland Plateau are oddly rich in prairie grasses such as big bluestem, Indian grass, and little bluestem; prairie forbs such as blazing-star and obedient plant also occur in profusion. This is presumably because the habitat, which was created by the sandy soil that is deposited among the interior boulders, in combination with extreme drought conditions, is similar to that in prairies. These cobble-bar communities develop under some of the toughest conditions and yet are very fragile. Alteration of the volume, periodicity of river flow, or soil deposition from erosion of the land around these systems will cause decline in quality and an invasion of weed flora. To remain ecologically healthy, the watershed of

Rockcastle aster is a state threatened species that grows in between cobble bars and forest slopes.

rivers, especially those with cobble-bar habitat, should remain forested, at least along their slopes and tributaries.

Virginia spiraea, a federal- and state-listed shrub, occurs on these bars and riverbanks. This shrub can create large, impenetrable masses of woody stems. A strong flood may wipe out these masses of stems but leave the root systems intact, and the plants start over as pencil-thin ground shoots. This adaptation allows this species to withstand the kinds of floods that occur only once or twice in a century. Unfortunately, Virginia spiraea does not regularly produce seed, perhaps because the populations have become so small and isolated.

Three other rare species that are characteristic of cobble-bar habitat are Cumberland rosemary, Barbara's-buttons, and Rockcastle aster. They grow only in the sandy deposits among the boulders. Cumberland rosemary is a low evergreen shrub in the mint family. The decline of this federally listed species in Kentucky is hard to explain because it is found on one of the most pristine rivers in the state, the Big South Fork. These three species are vulnerable to collection since they are all beautiful plants; additionally, they have endured both natural and human-caused disturbances. One of the threats to these plants is all-terrain vehicle (ATV) use along rivers and their adjacent slopes. The trails cause the soil to loosen and move downslope, where its deposition causes changes in the flora, including an invitation to weeds.

The rare plants in streams and rivers, many of which can be seen in the following photographs, are found in habitats from dry, sandy deposits among boulders to river shores.

Spiked hoary pea 🌸 Spiked hoary pea occurs in sandy deposits of river cobble bars and upland sandy grasslands in eastern Kentucky.

Shining ladies'-tresses 🌸 Shining ladies'-tresses is the earliest blooming of the ladies'-tresses orchids. Its habitat is moist shores, which in Kentucky are primarily alongside streams, and it is therefore vulnerable to soil compaction, trampling, or changes in water level or flow.

American barberry 🔹 American barberry is a host for a rust fungus that has infected wheat crops for hundreds of years. Because it is uniquely suited to assist the rust in completing its life cycle, barberry species (many of which were introduced from Europe) were systematically eliminated in some parts of the country through a federal program, although Kentucky was not included in that program. It is native to the middle-eastern states. It naturally occurs on rocky stream banks.

Virginia mallow Virginia mallow occurs along the Ohio River in open, sandy areas on riverbanks and terraces.

Eastern sweetshrub Eastern sweetshrub has aromatic foliage, and the dark red flowers smell like ripe strawberries. For this reason, this native shrub, found in southeastern Kentucky, is popular for gardens.

Trepocarpus Found on exposed shorelines, trepocarpus is a winter annual and a transient species that appears wherever this aquatic-terrestrial eco-zone develops.

Brook saxifrage ◦ Brook saxifrage occurs in crowded colonies on rocks in mountain streams in Kentucky. It is limited to the southeastern corner of the state.

Sand grape ◦ Sand grape seems to occur on the leeward side of river gravel bars, a precarious and dynamic habitat. The red stems of this grape are distinctive.

Sweet fern   Sweet fern is an aromatic, low-growing shrub—not a fern. The plants shown here represent almost the entire population of this species in the state.

Rand's goldenrod   Rand's goldenrod occurs on cobble bars along larger rivers in southeastern Kentucky.

Wetlands

Wetland floras are often dynamic, especially those in marshes. Species appear and disappear. As the hydrology changes, the plants respond, and one plant will take over and then another. Because many wetland communities are isolated, the dispersal from one to another is commonly through birds. It seems unlikely that a piece of plant or seed can make it to the next wetland by way of a bird—but dispersal happens. Sometimes it is difficult to distinguish between a plant that is a waif, like a single introduction from a bird foot or gut, and a species that has integrated itself into the state's flora. To be considered part of the Kentucky flora, a plant must be able to persist over seasons and years, including the coldest winters and the hottest drought periods.

Rare plants of wetlands are one of the largest groups of rare plants in the state. As might be expected, many of the rare wetland plants occur in western Kentucky, where flat land and therefore wetlands are more common. Twenty-five of the wetland species of conservation concern are from the westernmost natural regions. Some are submerged aquatics, such as Carolina fanwort, and others, such as frog's-bit, are above the water surface for most of the year. One common plant adaptation to living in water is an enlarged cell structure, so that the tissues contain more air; this allows them to float. Frog's-bit has a pocket of this tissue at the base of the leaf blade that it uses as a flotation device. This is the same device used by

A deepwater cypress swamp in Ballard County, near the confluence of the Ohio and Mississippi rivers.

Copper iris occurs only in the wetlands of far western Kentucky.

(right) Water locust is at the northern edge of its range.

(below) American frog's-bit is the floating leaf plant shown here with featherfoil.

greater bladderwort, which has splayed leaves that float and a flowering stalk that extends above the water. Bladderworts are carnivorous plants: tiny insects are trapped in the little bladders that are characteristic of this plant family and are digested, presumably as a source of nitrogen.

Copper iris is a perennial with a coastal plain distribution that barely reaches Kentucky. The reddish color of the regal-looking iris flowers attracts insects and hummingbirds and, of course, gardeners. Fortunately, this species is no longer particularly vulnerable to collection because it has been in the horticultural trade for so long.

Two rare wetland trees overlap in range in western Kentucky: water hickory and water locust. The former ranges into

Yellow-crested orchid is a smaller version of the more common yellow fringed orchid.

The white form of grass pink.

the northeastern United States, and the latter occurs to the south. Water hickory has flattish nuts and, although the meat is bitter, is loved by wildlife, since there are many fewer herbs in wetlands' groundcover. Water locust is one of many legumes that require special soil bacteria to thrive and produce nitrogen.

Wild rice occurs in western wetlands as well. In northern areas, where this grass is more common, harvest and use of wild rice is part of Native American culture, and it is often served with game. It is a little like tobacco for Kentuckians in that they can make extra money harvesting wild rice.

In forested wetlands with groundwater exuding at the surface, the persistent groundwater inhibits the establishment of

Grass pink is known from only one location in the state.

Nuttall's lobelia is a wet meadow species.

woody plants, and gaps form in the canopy. As is true in most natural places, the more light, the more plant diversity. These small openings create a splash of diversity in the otherwise continuously forested system. This is where a lot of Kentucky's terrestrial orchids are found, including several that are very rare, such as white fringeless orchid and yellow-crested orchid. White fringeless orchid is being considered for federal listing because of decreasing numbers caused by habitat decline. Another wetland orchid, grass pink, was found but has disappeared from several sites in the last 20 years; it is now known somewhat reliably in only a single place.

An endangered and delicate associate of the orchids in these seeps is Nuttall's lobelia. It is both narcotic and poisonous, as are all lobelia species. It occurs in wetlands throughout the Atlantic Gulf Coastal Plain (from Ellis Island to the Florida panhandle) and west to Kentucky.

Kentucky lady's-slipper usually is associated with the floodplains of midsize streams. Walking through a forest and coming upon a knee-high orchid with flowers as big as a baseball is a thrill whether you are a botanist or not. Arkansas and Tennessee actually have more Kentucky lady's-slipper than Kentucky, and it appears to be declining in this state. Certainly this is something that should concern Kentuckians. Orchids are under pressure not only from the ubiquitous loss of habitat but also from collection. These are very complex organisms that do not easily transplant because a particular type of soil fungus must be present for root establishment. In fact, commercially available orchids are commonly propagated by tissue culture, the growth of one plant from the tissue of another. The life history of orchids, from seed dispersal to seed establishment, seems so fabulous that it is hard to believe that, as a group, they have been successful (4,000 or so in tropical Ecuador and 42 in Kentucky). In addition to the highly specialized habitat requirements of many orchids, the seeds that are eventually produced are nearly microscopic. One fruiting capsule has thousands of seeds that rely on wind to carry them across the landscape; a few may miraculously land on suitable soil.

Another rare beauty of wetlands, grass-of-parnassus, is associated with calcareous (limestone) seeps. It is rare through-

The pollination of many orchids is highly specialized and provides a vivid example of the delicate process of species adaptation. The pollination mechanism for some species is so customized that only a single insect can be effective. Kentucky orchids generally have more than one possible pollinator. Lady's-slipper orchids attract several different insects, but bees tend to be the most successful at spreading pollen. The bee is lured to the flower by nectar guides that appear as stripes on the insect runway, the lip that leads to the flower throat. These landing guides have compounds that are visible as ultraviolet rays to insects. A bee crawls down the throat, which has downward pointing hairs, and falls—like Alice in Wonderland—into a pouch. There is no way out, except for some windows at the top of the pouch. The downward-pointing hairs prevent the bee's crawling back up the tunnel. As the bee leaves through the flower window, pollen is deposited like a saddlebag somewhere on its head or body. The odd thing is that there is no reward for the insect. Many flowers provide nectar for the insects, but these orchids, which must rely on the bees, do not. These are probably young, inexperienced bees that are being lured into the flowers over and over again with no real advantage to themselves.

Large-leaf grass-of-parnassus leaves have a narrow base and expand to a heart shape at the end.

Poison sumac.

Both of the grass-of-parnassus species in Kentucky occur in wetland seeps, have southeastern U.S. ranges, have fewer than three recorded locations, and occur near the southern border of the state. Kidney-leaf grass-of-parnassus has very rounded leaves.

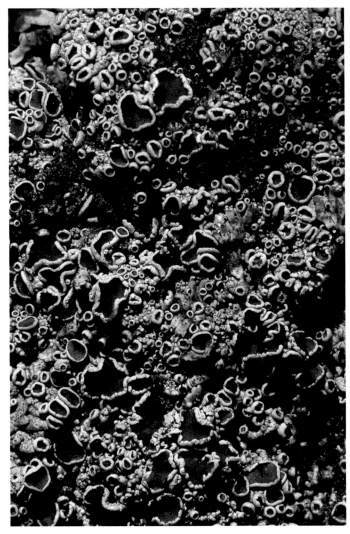

Lea's bog lichen is known only from tributaries of the Ohio River from Tennessee to northern Kentucky.

out its range, which is the southern United States as far north as Missouri. A single occurrence has been found in Kentucky.

Poison sumac, as you might guess, causes allergic reactions similar to its cousin, poison ivy. It is unlikely you will run into this rare wetland tree since there have been only two reports of it in the state, both in the east. This family, *Anacardiaceae,* is primarily tropical; it includes cashews and mangoes, which also contain the latex that causes an allergic reaction (although not when well washed). Another group in this family, including the rest of Kentucky's sumacs, does not have this poisonous latex.

Lichens are not plants, although they are grouped with them on the state's rare plant list. They result when an alga and a fungus combine to form a unique organism. Lichens are common in most habitats but are not thought of as being flood tolerant. Lea's bog lichen, however, is found exclusively in bottomland hardwood forests, and it occurs on the portion of tree trunks that is submerged. One possible reason for the decline of this lichen is the change in hydrology of the Ohio River as a result of dam construction.

Here are a few of the wetland plants that are considered rare in Kentucky.

Spoon-leaved sundew An unlikely-looking carnivorous plant three to five inches tall, this sundew captures insects with sticky glandular leaves. The plant dissolves the insects and presumably uses them as a source of nitrogen.

Dwarf sundew Dwarf sundew is about an inch or two tall and wide, yet it still manages to capture tiny insects as a nutrient source on its sticky glandular leaves. It is endangered in Kentucky.

Yellow screwstem Among the smallest plants in Kentucky, this species is associated with small depressions in forested wetlands as well as dry slopes on Pine Mountain.

Eastern featherbells Eastern featherbells may be confused with a grass until it flowers, and then the difference is striking. The flowering stem can be up to six feet tall. It is related to the lilies.

Blue-flower coyote-thistle The small, open wetlands where blue-flower coyote-thistle occurs have dramatically declined because of changes in hydrology and land use. The flowering heads of this species, similar but unrelated to thistles, comprise many tiny flowers.

Tennessee aster   Tennessee aster is known only from a small area of remnant dry pineland on Kentucky Lake that has been subdivided into house lots. The flower heads (made up of many small flowers) are especially large. This species is also known in highland rim wet meadows.

Shaggy hedge hyssop Shaggy hedge hyssop is a small member of the snapdragon family that occurs in low, wet openings. All species in this genus are avoided by cattle, presumably because of their bitter taste.

Short's hedge hyssop Short's hedge hyssop's stems are a little sticky because of glandular hairs. These hairs probably deter insects such as aphids, which cause damage by sucking fluids from plants.

Cross-leaf milkwort Cross-leaf milkwort is a few inches high and occurs on the acidic soils of open, wet prairies, wetlands that are rapidly disappearing. The flowers are crowded into a head, although each individual flower has the wing petals typical of the milkworts.

Virginia bunchflower 🌸 Despite its wide range in the eastern and central United States, Virginia bunchflower is endangered in Kentucky. This wetland plant is related to the lily family.

Round-headed bush clover 🌸 Round-headed bush clover is a silver-leaved prairie species most common in the Midwest. It is nutritious forage for mammals of all kinds, and the seeds are a good food source for wildlife. It can be found in mesic to wet grasslands.

Swamp candle   Swamp candles, named for their bright yellow floral display, have not been seen in Kentucky wetlands for many years.

Saint-Peter's-wort   Saint-Peter's-wort is found in open, sandy, acidic meadows in Kentucky. This genus of plants, *Hypericum* (also known as Saint-John's-wort), has been used to develop antidepressant medications.

Mock bishop's weed This annual takes advantage of exposed ground in wetland systems to establish itself; it then may disappear once other species take over the habitat.

Hairy ludwigia Hairy ludwigia is currently known to exist in a single site in Kentucky.

Silphium sunflower   Silphium sunflower is found on acid, sandy soils
near swamps on the far western border of Kentucky.

Vetchling peavine   Though vetchling peavine has a circumboreal range (that is, it is widely distributed in northern temperate regions), it is a rare plant in Kentucky, found only on stream banks. Like many legumes, it concentrates nitrogen in the soil.

Slender marsh pink ❧ Slender marsh pink is a plant of wet meadows in eastern Kentucky.

Eastern bluestar ❧ This variety of eastern bluestar occurs in only three states: Tennessee, Kentucky, and Mississippi.

Carolina yellow-eyed grass Carolina yellow-eyed grass is in the genus *Xyris,* a mostly tropical group of plants. It is primarily a southeastern U.S. species, though a few occur in the north. The flowers usually emerge in the morning and are insect pollinated.

Sweetscent ladies'-tresses There are 42 species of native orchids in the state, and this fragrant ladies'-tresses is one of the few that bloom in the fall.

American golden-saxifrage   American golden-saxifrage is not a saxifrage, although related, and it has no flower petals. A nectar disc dominates the center of the tiny flower on this little plant. It is also called water carpet because it creeps across wet, shady areas.

Tawny cotton-grass   Tawny cotton-grass is a northern species of wet meadows and bogs that just reaches Kentucky. It is widely scattered in the eastern part of the state.

Northern bog club-moss   As may be predicted, northern bog club-moss is known from Kentucky's Cumberland Mountains, an area with a concentration of species with northern affinities. Club-mosses are simple, creeping plants that reproduce by spores and do not form flowers.

Cypress-swamp sedge   Cypress-swamp sedge doesn't occur in cypress swamps in Kentucky. Oddly, it is associated with shallow, wet depressions in eastern Kentucky, a habitat different from those in more southern states.

Rose turtlehead   There are two varieties of pink turtlehead occurring at opposite ends of the state. This variety lives in cypress and bottomland hardwood swamps and the other in swamps in eastern Kentucky.

Grassleaf mud-plantain Grassleaf mud-plantain inhabits mudflats. When submersed, the flowering plants look like yellow stars on the water's surface. The plant is reported to occur nationwide, although it is rare in some states.

Pickerel-weed The blue-flowered spikes of pickerel-weed are usually heavily visited by bees for their nectar. This wetland plant is associated with pond margins or slow-moving waters. Both the young leaves and the fruit are edible.

Ovate false fiddleleaf Ovate false fiddleleaf occurs in shallow pools in wetlands in western Kentucky. Many of the reported occurrences for this species are now extirpated.

Floating pennywort ⧫ Floating pennywort forms large, floating mats in marshes.

Narrow-leaved meadowsweet ⧫ This small shrub is more common in northeastern states. It has not been seen in Kentucky for some years.

Hoary azalea   Hoary azalea is associated with swamps in the Coastal Plain of Kentucky. The species has been bred for the horticultural trade, as are many rhododendron species.

Large bur-reed Large bur-reed is in a family of plants similar to cattails and widely distributed in North America. There are two species in Kentucky. The entire plant is used by wildlife, including muskrats, deer, waterfowl, and beavers.

Cliff Lines and Rockhouses

Most rare plants adapted to cliff lines occur exclusively in these dry, rocky habitats. There are roughly a dozen species on the rare plant list that are cliff dwellers.

Starting in the east, a couple of these rare plants occur on the high mountain ridge that divides Virginia and Kentucky. Silverling is rare throughout most of its basically Appalachian range, although there are occurrences in several Atlantic coastal states. Two related grasses, both limited to cliffs, are tufted hairgrass, a high-elevation species of the Cumberland Mountains, and crinkled hairgrass, which is found only along the limestone ledges of the Kentucky Palisades. Svenson's wild rye, another grass associated with the rock outcrops along the high hills of the Kentucky River, is distinctive in that the long, stiff hair on its fruit dramatically curls back on itself. This is another species, like Braun's rock-cress, that is disjunct with the Nashville area. It is distributed from Mercer County north to Owen County.

Something else that is cropping up along the Palisades is houses. Understandably, people want to have a beautiful view of the river valley from their homes, but these houses can destabilize the cliff habitat. Even those that are not directly on the Palisades can result in increased erosion and weedy invasions that lead to a decline of the forest quality and the cliff-line communities.

Cleft phlox has needlelike leaves that allow the plant to conserve moisture on the exposed rock of the Kentucky Palisades. The flowers are as pretty as any phlox and also have a slight cleft in the blue-lavender petals. Cleft phlox is another species that is disjunct between the Bluegrass region and the Nashville Basin region.

Several of the plants in these natural communities are

Silverling.

Allegheny stonecrop occurs along cliffs in western Kentucky and flowers in October.

Svenson's wild rye is a limestone cliff species.

Cleft phlox occurs along the Kentucky River Palisades.

tiny by any measure. Two sandworts have threadlike stalks that support tiny white flowers. Hundreds of sandwort plants may clump in a pin-cushion shape. One species, Appalachian sandwort, is typically on cliff tops, and the other, Cumberland sandwort, is known from a single location near the Tennessee border.

Allegheny stonecrop is found in western Kentucky counties near the Ohio River. All the species in the family (*Crassulaceae*) are succulent, and several related species have been used in xeriscape (water conserving) landscaping because they adapt so well to dry places. Unlike most of the other plants in this habitat, this species is not diminutive but is typically a foot or taller—which is remarkable considering that it is anchored in a small amount of soil that has accumulated on open rock. The flowers of this species vary from pink to a brilliant red.

All the following photographs show plants that occur exclusively in cliff-line and rockhouse habitats in Kentucky.

Walter's violet Walter's violet is associated with limestone cliffs in Kentucky.

Lucy Braun's white snakeroot 🌿 Lucy Braun's white snakeroot occurs in rockhouses—depressions or shallow caves in the sides of forested slopes. It is concentrated around the drip line, the area where water runs off the upper slope to the rockhouse floor.

French's shooting star 🌿 French's shooting star, a sandstone rockhouse species, has distinctive leaves that abruptly taper to a narrow base.

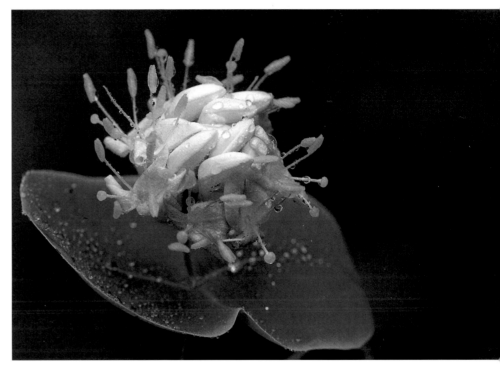

Grape honeysuckle The leaves of grape honeysuckle completely encircle the stem; it is a woody vine much different from the infamous exotic bush honeysuckle.

Ground juniper Ground juniper differs from red cedar in having whorled leaves with a joint at the base, and it remains a shrub generally well under six feet tall. It is most commonly found on cliffs.

Canby's mountain-lover 🍂 Canby's mountain-lover is a diminutive woody evergreen found on widely scattered limestone ridges from Carter to Wayne counties in Kentucky. It has been speculated that the clonal nature of this species, combined with the isolation of its occurrences, has resulted in populations that are basically all one individual.

Plant Names Appearing in the Text

Acer negundo L.	box elder
Acer rubrum L.	red maple
Acer saccharinum L.	silver maple
Acer saccharum Marsh.	sugar maple
Aesculus flava Ait.	yellow buckeye
Aesculus glabra Willd.	Ohio buckeye
Aesculus pavia L.	dwarf red buckeye
Ambrosia artemisiifolia L.	annual ragweed
Andropogon gerardii Vitman	big bluestem
Andropogon gyrans Ashe	Elliott's broom sedge
Aquilegia canadensis L.	columbine
Arisaema triphyllum (L.) Schott	jack-in-the-pulpit
Aristolochia macrophylla Lam.	pipe-vine
Asclepias incarnata L.	swamp milkweed
Asimina triloba (L.) Dunal	pawpaw
Asplenium bradleyi D.C. Eat.	Bradley's spleenwort
Asplenium montanum Willd.	mountain spleenwort
Asplenium pinnatifidum Nutt.	lobed spleenwort
Asplenium rhizophyllum L.	walking fern
Asplenium trichomanes L.	maidenhair spleenwort
Athyrium filix-femina (L.) Roth	common lady fern
Betula alleghaniensis Britt.	yellow birch
Betula nigra L.	river birch
Bidens discoidea (Torr. & Gray) Britt.	few-branched beggar-ticks
Bignonia capreolata L.	crossvine
Boehmeria cylindrica (L.) Sw.	smallspike false nettle
Campsis radicans (L.) Seem. ex Bureau	trumpet creeper
Carya cordiformis (Wangenh.) K. Koch	bitternut hickory
Carya glabra (P. Mill.) Sweet	pignut hickory
Carya illinoinensis (Wangenh.) K. Koch	pecan
Carya ovata (P. Mill.) K. Koch	shagbark hickory
Celastrus scandens L.	American bittersweet
Cephalanthus occidentalis L.	common buttonbush
Cercis canadensis L.	eastern redbud
Cheilanthes lanosa (Michx.) D.C. Eat.	hairy lip fern
Chelone glabra L.	white turtlehead
Chimaphila maculata (L.) Pursh	spotted wintergreen
Claytonia spp. L.	spring beauty
Clethra acuminata Michx.	mountain sweet pepperbush
Coreopsis major Walt.	greater tickseed
Coreopsis tripteris L.	tall tickseed
Crotonopsis elliptica Willd.	rushfoil
Cystopteris bulbifera (L.) Bernh.	bulblet bladder fern
Cystopteris tennesseensis Shaver	Tennessee bladder fern
Danthonia spicata (L.) Beauv. ex Roemer & J.A. Schultes	curly grass
Dodecatheon meadia L.	shooting star
Dryopteris intermedia (Muhl. ex Willd.) Gray	intermediate wood fern
Echinacea simulata R.L. McGregor	pale purple coneflower
Epigaea repens L.	trailing arbutus
Fagus grandifolia Ehrh.	American beech
Fraxinus americana L.	white ash
Fraxinus pennsylvanica Marsh.	green ash

Note: Rare plant names are listed separately, beginning on page 171.

Fraxinus quadrangulata Michx.	blue ash	*Paronychia canadensis* (L.) Wood	smooth-forked nailwort
Helianthus angustifolius L.	swamp sunflower	*Parthenocissus quinquefolia* (L.) Planch.	Virginia creeper
Heliotropium tenellum (Nutt.) Torr.	heliotrope	*Pellaea atropurpurea* (L.) Link	purple cliffbrake
Heuchera parviflora Bartl.	little-flowered alum-root	*Pellaea glabella* Mett. ex Kuhn	smooth cliffbrake
Heuchera villosa Michx.	hairy alum-root	*Phlox glaberrima* L.	smooth phlox
Hibiscus moscheutos L.	rose-mallow	*Phlox pilosa* L.	prairie phlox
Hydrangea arborescens L.	wild hydrangea	*Physostegia virginiana* (L.) Benth.	obedient plant
Hypericum gentianoides (L.) B.S.P.	orange-grass	*Pilea pumila* (L.) Gray	clearweed
Hypoxis hirsuta (L.) Coville	yellow star-grass	*Pinus echinata* P. Mill.	shortleaf pine
Itea virginica L.	Virginia willow	*Pinus rigida* P. Mill.	pitch pine
Juglans nigra L.	black walnut	*Pinus strobus* L.	eastern white pine
Juniperus virginiana L.	eastern red cedar	*Pityopsis graminifolia* (Michx.) Nutt.	grass-leaved golden-aster
Justicia americana (L.) Vahl	American water-willow	*Platanus occidentalis* L.	American sycamore
Kalmia latifolia L.	mountain laurel	*Polygonum* spp. L.	smartweed
Krigia virginica (L.) Willd.	Virginia dwarf-dandelion	*Polygonum sagittatum* L.	arrow-leaved tearthumb
Lechea tenuifolia Michx.	narrowleaf pinweed	*Polypodium virginianum* L.	rock polypody
Lemna minor L.	common duckweed	*Populus deltoides* Bartr. ex Marsh.	eastern cottonwood
Liatris spp. Gaertn. ex Schreb.	blazing-star	*Populus heterophylla* L.	swamp cottonwood
Liatris spicata (L.) Willd.	spiked blazing-star	*Potamogeton diversifolius* Raf.	snailseed pondweed
Lindera benzoin (L.) Blume	northern spicebush	*Prenanthes racemosa* Michx.	purple rattlesnake-root
Liquidambar styraciflua L.	sweetgum	*Prunus serotina* Ehrh.	black cherry
Liriodendron tulipifera L.	tuliptree	*Pyrularia pubera* Michx.	buffalo-nut
Lithospermum canescens (Michx.) Lehm.	hoary puccoon	*Quercus alba* L.	white oak
Lobelia cardinalis L.	cardinal-flower	*Quercus coccinea* Muenchh.	scarlet oak
Magnolia acuminata (L.) L.	cucumber-tree	*Quercus falcata* Michx.	southern red oak
Magnolia fraseri Walt.	mountain magnolia	*Quercus lyrata* Walt.	overcup oak
Maianthemum racemosum (L.) Link	false Solomon's seal	*Quercus macrocarpa* Michx.	bur oak
Manfreda virginica (L.) Salisb. ex Rose	false aloe	*Quercus marilandica* Muenchh.	blackjack oak
Medeola virginiana L.	Indian cucumber	*Quercus muehlenbergii* Engelm.	chinkapin oak
Mertensia virginica (L.) Pers. ex Link	Virginia bluebells	*Quercus palustris* Muenchh.	pin oak
Nyssa aquatica L.	water tupelo	*Quercus phellos* L.	willow oak
Nyssa sylvatica Marsh.	black gum	*Quercus prinus* L.	chestnut oak
Opuntia humifusa (Raf.) Raf.	prickly-pear cactus	*Quercus shumardii* Buckl.	Shumard's oak
Osmunda cinnamomea L.	cinnamon fern	*Quercus stellata* Wangenh.	post oak
Osmunda regalis L.	royal fern	*Quercus velutina* Lam.	black oak
Oxydendrum arboreum (L.) DC.	sourwood	*Ratibida pinnata* (Vent.) Barnh.	prairie or yellow coneflower
Panicum virgatum L.	switchgrass	*Rhododendron catawbiense* Michx.	mountain rosebay
Parietaria pensylvanica Muhl. ex Willd.	Pennsylvania pellitory	*Rhododendron maximum* L.	great rhododendron

Rhus aromatica Ait.	fragrant sumac
Rhus copallinum L.	winged sumac
Rhynchospora corniculata (Lam.) Gray	shortbristle beak-rush
Rosa palustris Marsh.	swamp rose
Salix nigra Marsh.	black willow
Sanguinaria canadensis L.	bloodroot
Saxifraga virginiensis Michx.	early saxifrage
Schizachyrium scoparium (Michx.) Nash	little bluestem
Scutellaria parvula Michx.	small skullcap
Sedum pulchellum Michx.	widow's-cross
Sedum ternatum Michx.	woodland stonecrop
Silene caroliniana Walt.	sticky catchfly
Silphium terebinthinaceum Jacq.	prairie rosinweed or prairie dock
Sorghastrum nutans (L.) Nash	Indian grass
Sparganium americanum Nutt.	American bur-reed
Spartina pectinata Bosc ex Link	prairie cord grass
Sporobolus compositus (Poir.) Merr.	tall dropseed
Sporobolus vaginiflorus (Torr. ex Gray) Wood	poverty dropseed
Staphylea trifolia L.	American bladdernut
Stylophorum diphyllum (Michx.) Nutt.	wood or celandine poppy
Taxodium distichum (L.) L.C. Rich.	bald cypress
Thalictrum mirabile Small	little mountain meadow-rue
Tilia americana L. var. *heterophylla* (Vent.) Loud.	white basswood
Toxicodendron radicans (L.) Kuntze	eastern poison ivy
Triadenum walteri (J.G. Gmel.) Gleason	greater marsh Saint-John's-wort
Trichomanes boschianum Sturm	Appalachian filmy fern
Trichostema dichotomum L.	forked blue-curls
Trillium grandiflorum (Michx.) Salisb.	large-flowered trillium
Tripsacum dactyloides (L.) L.	eastern gama-grass
Tsuga canadensis (L.) Carr.	eastern hemlock
Typha latifolia L.	common cattail
Ulmus alata Michx.	winged elm
Ulmus americana L.	American elm
Utricularia inflata Walter	swollen bladderwort
Vaccinium stamineum L.	farkleberry
Viburnum acerifolium L.	mapleleaf viburnum
Viola blanda Willd.	sweet white violet
Vitis aestivalis Michx.	summer grape
Vitis vulpina L.	fox grape

Rare and Extirpated Plants of Kentucky

The Kentucky State Nature Preserves Commission updates the list of rare and extirpated or extinct plants for the state. The list here includes one lichen and 390 plants considered rare in Kentucky, as well as 6 plants considered extirpated from Kentucky, or extinct. (*Extinct* or *extirpated* refers to a taxon for which habitat loss has been pervasive, or concerted efforts by knowledgeable biologists to collect or observe specimens within appropriate habitats have failed. An extinct taxon is one that no longer exists. An extirpated taxon is one that no longer exists in the wild in Kentucky but exists elsewhere in the wild.)

Codes

E: Endangered. A taxon in danger of extirpation or extinction throughout all or a significant part of its range in Kentucky.

T: Threatened. A taxon likely to become endangered within the near future throughout all or a significant part of its range in Kentucky.

S: Special Concern. A taxon that should be monitored because (1) it exists in a limited geographic area in Kentucky, (2) it may become threatened or endangered owing to modification or destruction of habitat, (3) certain characteristics or requirements make it especially vulnerable to specific pressures, (4) experienced researchers have identified other factors that may jeopardize it, or (5) it is thought to be rare or declining in Kentucky but insufficient information exists for assignment to the threatened or endangered status categories.

H: Historic. A taxon documented from Kentucky, but not observed reliably since 1984 and not considered extinct or extirpated.

Alabama lip fern	*Cheilanthes alabamensis*	H
Alder-leaved viburnum	*Viburnum lantanoides*	E
Allegheny chinkapin	*Castanea pumila*	T
Allegheny stonecrop	*Sedum telephioides*	T
Allegheny-vine	*Adlumia fungosa*	E
American barberry	*Berberis canadensis*	E
American chestnut	*Castanea dentata*	E
American cow-wheat	*Melampyrum lineare* var. *latifolium*	T
American cow-wheat	*Melampyrum lineare* var. *pectinatum*	E
American frog's-bit	*Limnobium spongia*	T
American golden-saxifrage	*Chrysosplenium americanum*	T
American lily-of-the-valley	*Convallaria montana*	E
American speedwell	*Veronica americana*	H
American water-pennywort	*Hydrocotyle americana*	E
American wintergreen	*Pyrola americana*	H
Appalachian bugbane	*Cimicifuga rubifolia*	T
Appalachian bunchflower	*Veratrum parviflorum*	E
Appalachian rosinweed	*Silphium wasiotense*	S
Appalachian sandwort	*Minuartia glabra*	T
Appalachian sedge	*Carex appalachica*	T
Appalachian woodsia	*Woodsia scopulina* ssp. *appalachiana*	H
Barbara's-buttons	*Marshallia grandiflora*	E
Barbed rattlesnake-root	*Prenanthes barbata*	E
Barrens silky aster	*Symphyotrichum pratense*	S
Bashful bulrush	*Trichophorum planifolium*	E
Bay starvine	*Schisandra glabra*	E
Beaked yellow trout lily	*Erythronium rostratum*	S
Bearded skeleton grass	*Gymnopogon ambiguus*	S
Bent reed grass	*Calamagrostis porteri* ssp. *insperata*	E
Blackfoot quillwort	*Isoetes melanopoda*	E
Blue-flower coyote-thistle	*Eryngium integrifolium*	E
Blue jasmine leatherflower	*Clematis crispa*	T
Bluejoint reed grass	*Calamagrostis canadensis* var. *macouniana*	H
Blue monkshood	*Aconitum uncinatum*	T
Blue mud-plantain	*Heteranthera limosa*	S
Blue scorpion-weed	*Phacelia ranunculacea*	S
Blue wild indigo	*Baptisia australis* var. *minor*	S
Blunt-lobe grape fern	*Botrychium oneidense*	H
Blunt mountainmint	*Pycnanthemum muticum*	H
Bog rush	*Juncus elliottii*	H
Branched three-awn grass	*Aristida ramosissima*	H
Braun's rock-cress	*Arabis perstellata*	T
Bristly sedge	*Carex comosa*	H
Broad-leaf golden-aster	*Heterotheca subaxillaris* var. *latifolia*	T
Broadleaf water-milfoil	*Myriophyllum heterophyllum*	S
Broadwing sedge	*Carex alata*	T
Brook saxifrage	*Boykinia aconitifolia*	T
Brown bog sedge	*Carex buxbaumii*	H
Buckley's goldenrod	*Solidago buckleyi*	S
Buffalo clover	*Trifolium reflexum*	E
Bull paspalum	*Paspalum boscianum*	S
Burhead	*Echinodorus berteroi*	T
Bush's muhly	*Muhlenbergia bushii*	E
Butler's quillwort	*Isoetes butleri*	E
Canada burnet	*Sanguisorba canadensis*	E
Canada frostweed	*Helianthemum canadense*	E
Canada yew	*Taxus canadensis*	T
Canby's mountain-lover	*Paxistima canbyi*	T
Carolina anglepod	*Matelea carolinensis*	E
Carolina fanwort	*Cabomba caroliniana*	T
Carolina larkspur	*Delphinium carolinianum*	T
Carolina yellow-eyed grass	*Xyris difformis*	E
Cedar sedge	*Carex juniperorum*	E
Chaffseed	*Schwalbea americana*	H
Cleft phlox	*Phlox bifida* ssp. *bifida*	T
Clustered bluet	*Oldenlandia uniflora*	E

Clustered poppy-mallow	*Callirhoe alcaeoides*	H
Coastal plain sedge	*Carex crebriflora*	T
Common silverbell	*Halesia tetraptera*	E
Compass-plant	*Silphium laciniatum*	T
Conjurer's nut	*Nestronia umbellula*	E
Copper iris	*Iris fulva*	E
Cow-parsnip	*Heracleum lanatum*	H
Crawe's sedge	*Carex crawei*	S
Cream wild indigo	*Baptisia bracteata* var. *glabrescens*	S
Creeping Saint-John's-wort	*Hypericum adpressum*	H
Crinkled hairgrass	*Deschampsia flexuosa*	T
Cross-leaf milkwort	*Polygala cruciata*	E
Cumberland rosemary	*Conradina verticillata*	E
Cumberland sandwort	*Minuartia cumberlandensis*	E
Curtis' goldenrod	*Solidago curtisii*	T
Cutleaf meadow-parsnip	*Thaspium pinnatifidum*	T
Cutleaf water-milfoil	*Myriophyllum pinnatum*	H
Cypress-swamp sedge	*Carex joorii*	E
Delta arrowhead	*Sagittaria platyphylla*	T
Downy arrowwood	*Viburnum rafinesquianum* var. *rafinesquianum*	T
Downy goldenrod	*Solidago puberula*	S
Drooping blue grass	*Poa saltuensis*	E
Dwarf burhead	*Echinodorus parvulus*	E
Dwarf sundew	*Drosera brevifolia*	E
Ear-leaf false foxglove	*Agalinis auriculata*	E
Eastern bluestar	*Amsonia tabernaemontana* var. *gattingeri*	E
Eastern featherbells	*Stenanthium gramineum*	T
Eastern mock bishop's weed	*Ptilimnium costatum*	H
Eastern silvery aster	*Symphyotrichum concolor*	T
Eastern sweetshrub	*Calycanthus floridus* var. *glaucus*	T
Eastern turkey-beard	*Xerophyllum asphodeloides*	H
Eastern waterleaf	*Hydrophyllum virginianum*	T
Eastern yampah	*Perideridia americana*	T
Eel grass	*Vallisneria americana*	S
Eggert's sunflower	*Helianthus eggertii*	T
Eggleston's violet	*Viola septemloba* var. *egglestonii*	S
Epiphytic sedge	*Carex decomposita*	T
Epling's hedge-nettle	*Stachys eplingii*	H
Evening primrose	*Oenothera oakesiana*	H
Fee's lip fern	*Cheilanthes feei*	E
Few-flowered scurfpea	*Psoralidium tenuiflorum*	H
Filmy angelica	*Angelica triquinata*	E
Finely-nerved sedge	*Carex leptonervia*	E
Floating pennywort	*Hydrocotyle ranunculoides*	E
Fly-poison	*Amianthium muscitoxicum*	T
Fraser's sedge	*Cymophyllus fraserianus*	E
French's shooting star	*Dodecatheon frenchii*	S
Fringed nut-rush	*Scleria ciliate*	E
Gattinger's lobelia	*Lobelia gattingeri*	E
Gaywings	*Polygala paucifolia*	E
Globe beak-rush	*Rhynchospora recognita*	S
Globe bladderpod	*Lesquerella globosa*	E
Goldenclub	*Orontium aquaticum*	T
Grape honeysuckle	*Lonicera prolifera*	E
Grassleaf mud-plantain	*Heteranthera dubia*	S
Grass-leaved arrowhead	*Sagittaria graminea*	T
Grass pink	*Calopogon tuberosus*	E
Great angelica	*Angelica atropurpurea*	E
Greater bladderwort	*Utricularia macrorhiza*	E
Great Plains ladies'-tresses	*Spiranthes magnicamporum*	T
Green-and-gold	*Chrysogonum virginianum*	E
Ground juniper	*Juniperus communis* var. *depressa*	T
Hairgrass	*Muhlenbergia glabrifloris*	S
Hairy false gromwell	*Onosmodium hispidissimum*	E
Hairy fimbristylis	*Fimbristylis puberula*	T
Hairy hawkweed	*Hieracium longipilum*	T
Hairy heart-leaved aster	*Symphyotrichum drummondii* var. *texanum*	H
Hairy ludwigia	*Ludwigia hirtella*	E
Hairy skullcap	*Scutellaria arguta*	E
Hairy snoutbean	*Rhynchosia tomentosa*	E
Hall's bulrush	*Schoenoplectus hallii*	E
Heart-leaved plantain	*Plantago cordata*	H

Hispid false mallow	*Malvastrum hispidum*	T
Hoary azalea	*Rhododendron canescens*	E
Hoary mock-orange	*Philadelphus pubescens*	E
Illinois pondweed	*Potamogeton illinoensis*	S
Indian wild rice	*Zizania palustris* var. *interior*	H
Jointed rush	*Juncus articulatus*	S
Kentucky glade cress	*Leavenworthia exigua* var. *laciniata*	E
Kentucky lady's-slipper	*Cypripedium kentuckiense*	E
Kidney-leaf grass-of-parnassus	*Parnassia asarifolia*	E
Kidney-leaf twayblade	*Listera smallii*	T
Lake cress	*Armoracia lacustris*	T
Large bur-reed	*Sparganium eurycarpum*	E
Large-leaf grass-of-parnassus	*Parnassia grandifolia*	E
Large sedge	*Carex gigantean*	T
Large spotted Saint-John's-wort	*Hypericum pseudomaculatum*	H
Least trillium	*Trillium pusillum*	E
Lescur's bladderpod	*Lesquerella lescurii*	H
Lesser rattlesnake-plantain	*Goodyera repens*	E
Lettuce-leaf saxifrage	*Saxifraga micranthidifolia*	E
Limestone fame-flower	*Talinum calcaricum*	E
Loesel's twayblade	*Liparis loeselii*	T
Long-bracted green orchid	*Coeloglossum viride* var. *virescens*	H
Longleaf stitchwort	*Stellaria longifolia*	S
Louisiana broomrape	*Orobanche ludoviciana*	H
Lucy Braun's white snakeroot	*Ageratina luciae-brauniae*	S
Matricary grape fern	*Botrychium matricariifolium*	E
Mercury spurge	*Euphorbia mercurialina*	T
Michaux's bluet	*Houstonia serpyllifolia*	E
Michaux's saxifrage	*Saxifraga michauxii*	T
Missouri rock-cress	*Arabis missouriensis*	H
Mock bishop's weed	*Ptilimnium capillaceum*	T
Mock-orange	*Philadelphus inodorus*	T
Mountain maple	*Acer spicatum*	E
Narrow-leaved blue-curls	*Trichostema setaceum*	E
Narrow-leaved meadowsweet	*Spiraea alba*	E
Necklace glade cress	*Leavenworthia torulosa*	T
Nettle-leaf noseburn	*Tragia urticifolia*	E
Nettle-leaf sage	*Salvia urticifolia*	E
Nodding rattlesnake-root	*Prenanthes crepidinea*	T
Northern bog club-moss	*Lycopodium inundatum*	E
Northern dropseed	*Sporobolus heterolepis*	E
Northern fox grape	*Vitis labrusca*	S
Northern starflower	*Trientalis borealis*	E
Northern white cedar	*Thuja occidentalis*	T
Northern witchgrass	*Dichanthelium boreale*	S
Nuttall's lobelia	*Lobelia nuttallii*	T
Nuttall's milkwort	*Polygala nuttallii*	H
Nuttall's mock bishop's weed	*Ptilimnium nuttallii*	E
Nuttall's oak	*Quercus texana*	T
One-flower fiddleleaf	*Hydrolea uniflora*	H
Ovate catchfly	*Silene ovata*	E
Ovate false fiddleleaf	*Hydrolea ovata*	E
Painted trillium	*Trillium undulatum*	T
Pale manna grass	*Torreyochloa pallida*	H
Pale umbrella-wort	*Mirabilis albida*	H
Peach-leaf willow	*Salix amygdaloides*	H
Pickerel-weed	*Pontederia cordata*	T
Plains frostweed	*Helianthemum bicknellii*	E
Plains muhly	*Muhlenbergia cuspidata*	T
Plukenet's cyperus	*Cyperus plukenetii*	H
Poison sumac	*Toxicodendron vernix*	E
Porcupine sedge	*Carex hystericina*	H
Porter's reed grass	*Calamagrostis porteri* ssp. *porteri*	T
Possumhaw	*Viburnum nudum*	E
Prairie gentian	*Gentiana puberulenta*	E
Prairie June grass	*Koeleria macrantha*	E
Prairie redroot	*Ceanothus herbaceus*	T
Price's aster	*Symphyotrichum priceae*	T
Price's potato bean	*Apios priceana*	E
Price's yellow wood-sorrel	*Oxalis macrantha*	H
Prickly bog sedge	*Carex atlantica* ssp. *capillacea*	E

Purple giant hyssop	*Agastache scrophulariifolia*	H
Purple oat	*Schizachne purpurascens*	T
Purple prairie-clover	*Dalea purpurea*	S
Purple sand grass	*Triplasis purpurea*	H
Pussy willow	*Salix discolor*	H
Pyramid magnolia	*Magnolia pyramidata*	H
Racemed milkwort	*Polygala polygama*	T
Rand's goldenrod	*Solidago randii*	S
Red buckeye	*Aesculus pavia*	T
Red elderberry	*Sambucus racemosa* ssp. *pubens*	E
Red turtlehead	*Chelone obliqua* var. *obliqua*	E
Red-twig doghobble	*Leucothoe recurva*	E
Reniform sedge	*Carex reniformis*	E
Rigid sedge	*Carex tetanica*	E
Ringseed rush	*Juncus filipendulus*	T
River bulrush	*Bolboschoenus fluviatilis*	E
Roan Mountain goldenrod	*Solidago roanensis*	T
Roan Mountain sedge	*Carex roanensis*	E
Rockcastle aster	*Eurybia saxicastellii*	T
Rock harlequin	*Corydalis sempervirens*	S
Rock skullcap	*Scutellaria saxatilis*	T
Rose mock-vervain	*Verbena canadensis*	H
Rose pogonia	*Pogonia ophioglossoides*	E
Rose turtlehead	*Chelone obliqua* var. *speciosa*	S
Rosy twisted stalk	*Streptopus lanceolatus*	E
Rough dropseed	*Sporobolus clandestinus*	T
Rough-leaved aster	*Eurybia radula*	E
Rough pennyroyal	*Hedeoma hispidum*	T
Rough rattlesnake-root	*Prenanthes aspera*	E
Round-headed bush clover	*Lespedeza capitata*	S
Roundleaf fame-flower	*Talinum teretifolium*	E
Royal catchfly	*Silene regia*	E
Running buffalo clover	*Trifolium stoloniferum*	T
Running pine	*Lycopodium clavatum*	E
Saint-Peter's-wort	*Hypericum crux-andreae*	T
Sand grape	*Vitis rupestris*	T
Sand-myrtle	*Leiophyllum buxifolium*	H
Satincurls	*Clematis catesbyana*	H
Scarlet Indian paintbrush	*Castilleja coccinea*	E
September elm	*Ulmus serotina*	S
Sessile-fruited arrowhead	*Sagittaria rigida*	E
Shaggy hedge hyssop	*Gratiola pilosa*	T
Sharp-scaled manna grass	*Glyceria acutiflora*	E
Shining ladies'-tresses	*Spiranthes lucida*	T
Shortleaf skeleton grass	*Gymnopogon brevifolius*	E
Short's goldenrod	*Solidago shortii*	E
Short's hedge hyssop	*Gratiola viscidula*	S
Showy gentian	*Gentiana decora*	S
Showy lady's-slipper	*Cypripedium reginae*	H
Side-oats grama	*Bouteloua curtipendula*	S
Silphium sunflower	*Helianthus silphioides*	E
Silverling	*Paronychia argyrocoma*	E
Slender blazing-star	*Liatris cylindracea*	T
Slender bulrush	*Schoenoplectus heterochaetus*	H
Slender marsh pink	*Sabatia campanulata*	E
Small enchanter's nightshade	*Circaea alpina*	S
Small-flower baby-blue-eyes	*Nemophila aphylla*	T
Small-flower thoroughwort	*Eupatorium semiserratum*	E
Small-fruit bulrush	*Scirpus microcarpus*	H
Small purple-fringed orchid	*Platanthera psycodes*	E
Small rabbit-tobacco	*Pseudognaphalium helleri* ssp. *micradenium*	H
Small sundrop	*Oenothera perennis*	E
Small white lady's-slipper	*Cypripedium candidum*	E
Small yellow lady's-slipper	*Cypripedium parviflorum* var. *parviflorum*	T
Smooth blackberry	*Rubus canadensis*	E
Smooth veiny peavine	*Lathyrus venosus*	S
Snowberry	*Symphoricarpos albus*	E
Snow squarestem	*Melanthera nivea*	S
Snow trillium	*Trillium nivale*	E
Soft-haired thermopsis	*Thermopsis mollis*	E
Soft-hairy false gromwell	*Onosmodium molle*	H
Softleaf arrowwood	*Viburnum molle*	T
Southern bog club-moss	*Lycopodiella appressa*	E
Southern bog goldenrod	*Solidago gracillima*	S

Southern heartleaf	*Hexastylis contracta*	E
Southern maidenhair fern	*Adiantum capillus-veneris*	T
Southern mountain cranberry	*Vaccinium erythrocarpum*	E
Southern shagbark hickory	*Carya carolinae-septentrionalis*	T
Southern shield wood fern	*Dryopteris ludoviciana*	H
Southern twayblade	*Listera australis*	H
Southern wild rice	*Zizaniopsis miliacea*	T
Spiked hoary pea	*Tephrosia spicata*	E
Spinulose wood fern	*Dryopteris carthusiana*	S
Spoon-leaved sundew	*Drosera intermedia*	E
Spotted beebalm	*Monarda punctata*	H
Spotted coral-root	*Corallorhiza maculata*	E
Spotted joe-pye weed	*Eupatorium maculatum*	E
Spotted mandarin	*Prosartes maculata*	S
Spotted pondweed	*Potamogeton pulcher*	T
Spreading false foxglove	*Aureolaria patula*	S
Squarrose goldenrod	*Solidago squarrosa*	H
Stalkgrain sedge	*Carex stipata* var. *maxima*	H
Starflower false Solomon's seal	*Maianthemum stellatum*	E
Starry cleft phlox	*Phlox bifida* ssp. *stellaria*	E
Star tickseed	*Coreopsis pubescens*	S
Steele's joe-pye weed	*Eupatorium steelei*	T
Stemless evening primrose	*Oenothera triloba*	T
Straw sedge	*Carex straminea*	T
Summer sedge	*Carex aestivalis*	E
Supple-jack	*Berchemia scandens*	T
Svenson's wild rye	*Elymus svensonii*	S
Swamp candle	*Lysimachia terrestris*	E
Swamp lousewort	*Pedicularis lanceolata*	H
Swamp saxifrage	*Saxifraga pensylvanica*	H
Swamp wedge grass	*Sphenopholis pensylvanica*	S
Sweet coneflower	*Rudbeckia subtomentosa*	E
Sweet fern	*Comptonia peregrina*	E
Sweet pinesap	*Monotropsis odorata*	T
Sweetscent ladies'-tresses	*Spiranthes odorata*	E
Tall beak-rush	*Rhynchospora macrostachya*	E
Tall bush clover	*Lespedeza stuevei*	S
Tall hairy groovebur	*Agrimonia gryposepala*	T
Tansy rosinweed	*Silphium pinnatifidum*	S
Tarheel sedge	*Carex austrocaroliniana*	S
Tawny cotton-grass	*Eriophorum virginicum*	E
Ten-lobe false foxglove	*Agalinis obtusifolia*	E
Tennessee aster	*Eurybia hemispherica*	E
Tennessee leafcup	*Polymnia laevigata*	E
Thread-foot	*Podostemum ceratophyllum*	S
Thread-leaf sundrops	*Oenothera linifolia*	E
Thread-like naiad	*Najas gracillima*	S
Trailing loosestrife	*Lysimachia radicans*	H
Trepocarpus	*Trepocarpus aethusae*	S
Tufted hairgrass	*Deschampsia cespitosa*	E
Turk's cap lily	*Lilium superbum*	T
Umbel-like sedge	*Carex rugosperma*	T
Upland privet	*Forestiera ligustrina*	T
Vetchling peavine	*Lathyrus palustris*	T
Virginia bunchflower	*Melanthium virginicum*	E
Virginia mallow	*Sida hermaphrodita*	S
Virginia spiraea	*Spiraea virginiana*	T
Walter's violet	*Viola walteri*	T
Water hickory	*Carya aquatica*	T
Water locust	*Gleditsia aquatica*	S
Water oak	*Quercus nigra*	T
Water-plantain spearwort	*Ranunculus ambigens*	S
Water-purslane	*Didiplis diandra*	S
Water stitchwort	*Sagina fontinalis*	T
Weak stellate sedge	*Carex seorsa*	S
Wedge-leaf whitlow-grass	*Draba cuneifolia*	E
Western dwarf-dandelion	*Krigia occidentalis*	E
Western false gromwell	*Onosmodium occidentale*	E
Western hairy rock-cress	*Arabis hirsuta*	T
Western waterweed	*Elodea nuttallii*	T
White fringeless orchid	*Platanthera integrilabia*	E
White-haired goldenrod	*Solidago albopilosa*	T

Whiteleaf mountainmint	*Pycnanthemum albescens*	E
White rattlesnake-root	*Prenanthes alba*	E
White walnut	*Juglans cinerea*	S
Whorled aster	*Oclemena acuminata*	T
Whorled horse-balm	*Collinsonia verticillata*	E
Wild honeysuckle	*Lonicera dioica* var. *orientalis*	H
Wild lily-of-the-valley	*Maianthemum canadense*	T
Wild sarsaparilla	*Aralia nudicaulis*	E
Woodland beak-rush	*Scirpus expansus*	E
Wood lily	*Lilium philadelphicum*	T
Wood's bunchflower	*Veratrum woodii*	T
Woolly sedge	*Carex pellita*	H
Yellow-crested orchid	*Platanthera cristata*	T
Yellow evening primrose	*Calylophus serrulatus*	H
Yellow gentian	*Gentiana flavida*	E
Yellow nodding ladies'-tresses	*Spiranthes ochroleuca*	T
Yellow screwstem	*Bartonia virginica*	T
Yellow spikerush	*Eleocharis flavescens*	S
Yellow wild indigo	*Baptisia tinctoria*	T

EXTIRPATED OR EXTINCT PLANTS

Canada anemone	*Anemone canadensis*
Fraser's loosestrife	*Lysimachia fraseri*
Marsh marigold	*Caltha palustris* var. *palustris*
Prairie parsley	*Polytaenia nuttallii*
Slender dragonhead	*Physostegia intermedia*
Stipuled scurfpea	*Orbexilum stipulatum*

MOSSES

A haircap moss	*Polytrichum pallidisetum*	T
Matted feather moss	*Brachythecium populeum*	E
Moss	*Anomodon rugelii*	T
Moss	*Bryum cyclophyllum*	E
Moss	*Bryum miniatum*	E
Moss	*Cirriphyllum piliferum*	T
Moss	*Dicranodontium asperulum*	E
Moss	*Entodon brevisetus*	E
Moss	*Herzogiella turfacea*	E
Moss	*Neckera pennata*	T
Moss	*Oncophorus raui*	E
Moss	*Orthotrichum diaphanum*	E
Moss	*Polytrichum strictum*	E
A sphagnum moss	*Sphagnum quinquefarium*	E
Tortula	*Tortula norvegica*	E
Wire fern moss	*Abietinella abietina*	T

LICHEN

Lea's bog lichen	*Phaeophyscia leana*	E

References

Braun, E. L. 1950. *Deciduous Forests of Eastern North America.* Philadelphia: Blakiston Books.

Buchmann, S. L., and G. P. Nabhan. 1996. *The Forgotten Pollinators.* Washington, D.C.: Island Press.

Center for Wildlife Law and Defenders of Wildlife. 1996. Saving biodiversity. Albuquerque: Defenders of Wildlife.

Cowardin, L. M., V. Carter, F. G. Golet, and E. T. LaRoe. 1979. Classification of wetlands and deepwater habitats of the United States. FSW/OBS-79/31. Washington, D.C.: U.S. Department of Interior, Fish and Wildlife Service, Office of Biological Service (reprinted 1992).

Grieve, M. 1931. *A Modern Herbal.* Reprint, New York: Hafner Press, 1974.

Heywood, J. 2006. Fueling our transportation future. *Scientific American* 295, no. 3:60–63.

Jones, R. L. 2005. *Plant Life of Kentucky.* Lexington: University of Kentucky Press.

Kaan Kurtural, S. Grape rootstocks for Kentucky vineyards. Hortfact No. 3113. Lexington: University of Kentucky Cooperative Extension Service.

Kellert, S. R., 1996. *The Value of Life: Biological Diversity and Human Society.* Washington D.C.: Island Press.

Kellert, S. R., and E. O. Wilson, eds. 1993. *The Biophilia Hypothesis.* Washington D.C.: Island Press.

Kentucky, State of. 1994. Kentucky Rare Plant Recognition Act. *Kentucky Revised Statute,* sec. 146.600, July 15.

Kentucky Department of Fish and Wildlife. 1991. *Happy Hunting Ground.* Frankfort, Ky.

Kentucky State Nature Preserves Commission. 2007. Kentucky Natural Heritage Database. Frankfort, Ky.

Kruckeberg, A. R., and D. Rabinowitz. 1985. Biological aspects of endemism in higher plants. *Annual Review of Ecology Systematics* 16:447–79.

Kuchler, A. W. 1964. Manual to accompany the map of potential vegetation of the conterminous United States. Special Publication No. 36. New York: American Geographical Society.

Markham, V. D., and N. Steinzor. 2006. U.S. National report on population and the environment. In *Housing Facts, Figures and Trends.* Washington D.C.: National Association of Home Builders.

Menges, E. 1995. Factors limiting fecundity and germination in small populations of *Silene regia* (Caryophyllaceae), a rare hummingbird-pollinated prairie forb. *American Midland Naturalist* 133:242–55.

Natural Resources Conservation Service. 1997. Natural Resources Inventory (NRI).

Natureserve. 2006. www.natureserve.org.

Orleans, S. 1998. *The Orchid Thief.* Reprint, New York: Ballantine Books, 2000.

Pavord, A. 1999. *The Tulip.* New York: Bloomsbury Publishing.

Quammen, D. 1996. *Song of the Dodo: Island Biogeography in the Age of Extinctions.* New York: Scribner.

Stix, G. 2006. A climate repair manual. *Scientific American* 60 (September): 47.

Stoutamire, W. P. 1974. Relationships of the purple-fringed

orchids *Platanthera psycodes* and *P. grandiflora. Brittonia* 26, no. 1 (January–March): 42–58.

United Nations. 2004. World population prospects: 2004 revision.

U.S. Dept. of Transportation. Distribution of vehicles and persons per household. www.fhwa.dot.gov.

U.S. Fish and Wildlife Service. 1992. Endangered Species Act of 1973 as amended through the 100th Congress. United States. Washington, D.C.: Government Printing Office.

———. 2004. Endangered and threatened wildlife and plants. 50 CFR 17.11, 17.12. Washington, D.C.

U.S. Geological Survey. 2006. Estimated use of water in the United States in 2000. www.pubs.usgs.gov.

———. 2006. Historical statistics for mineral and material commodities in the United States.

U.S. Government. 2005. Annual energy review 2005. Washington, D.C.: Energy Information Administration.

Wilcove, D. L., and L. L. Master. 2005. How many endangered species are there in the United States? *Frontiers in Ecology and the Environment* 3:414–20.

Wilson, E. O. 2002. *The Future of Life.* New York: Alfred A. Knopf.

Index

Page numbers in *italics* refer to photographs or material in their captions.

bison, 25, 29, 37, 58–60, 97, 98

bitternut hickory (*Carya cordiformis*), 24

black cherry (*Prunus serotina*), 24, 25

black gum (*Nyssa sylvatica*), 23, 24

blackjack oak (*Quercus marilandica*), 23, 25

Black Mountain, 22, 25, 49, *49*, 50

black oak (*Quercus velutina*), 23

black walnut (*Juglans nigra*), 24

black willow (*Salix nigra*), 31

bladdernut (*Staphylea trifolia*), 24

blazing-star (*Liatris*), 25, 28, 34, *103*, 124

bloodroot (*Sanguinaria canadensis*), 24, 49

blue ash (*Fraxinus quadrangulata*), 29

blue-flower coyote-thistle (*Eryngium integri-
folium*), *142*

Bluegrass mesophytic cane forest, 24–25

Bluegrass natural region, 21, *21*, 56, 58, 98

    cliff lines and, 161

    glades and, 25

    woodlands and, 29

Bluegrass savanna-woodland, 29, *29*

blue jasmine leatherflower (*Clematis crispa*), 74

Blue Licks, 97–98

blue monkshood (*Aconitum uncinatum*), 55, 56

blue scorpion-weed (*Phacelia rununculacea*),
59, 60

blue wild indigo (*Baptisia australis* var. *minor*),
102

blunt-lobed grape fern (*Botrychium oneidense*),
50, 174

bogs, 32

bottomland hardwood forests, 31

Bowling Green, 37, 100

box elder (*Acer negundo*), 31

Bradley's spleenwort (*Asplenium bradleyi*), 30

Braun, E. Lucy, 24, 50–51, 54, 97

Braun's cotton-grass, 54

Braun's rock-cress (*Arabis perstellata*), 8, 44, 58

brook saxifrage (*Boykinia aconitifolia*), 51, *130*

broomsedge, 27

Buchmann, S. L., 9

Buckley's goldenrod (*Solidago buckleyi*), 82

Buddhist religion, 13

buffalo, 25, 29, 37, 58–60, 97

buffalo clover (*Trifolium reflexum*), *91*

buffalo-nut (*Pyrularia pubera*), 24

bulblet bladder fern (*Cystopteris bulbifera*), 30

Bullitt County, 5, 11–12, *26*, 99

bulrushes, 32

bunchgrasses, 98

burning bush, 9

bur oak (*Quercus macrocarpa*), 29

bur-reed (*Sparganium*), 32

bush honeysuckle, 9

butternut, *88*

buttonbush (*Cephalanthus occidentalis*), 31

calcareous xeric woodlands, 29

camping, 10

Canada anemone (*Anemone canadensis*), 3

Canada burnet (*Sanguisorba canadensis*), 51, *71*

Canada frostweed (*Helianthemum canadense*),
49–50, *50*

Canada yew (*Taxus canadensis*), 16, 54

Canby's mountain-lover (*Paxistima canbyi*), 54,
166

canopy cover, 22, 24, 29, 136

carbon dioxide, 16

cardinal-flower (*Lobelia cardinalis*), 28, 34

carnivorous plants, 134

Carolina anglepod (*Matelea carolinensis*), *87*

Carolina fanwort (*Cabomba caroliniana*), 133

Carolina larkspur (*Delphinium carolinianum*),
100, 100–101

Carolina yellow-eyed grass (*Xyris difformis*),
152

Catawba rhododendron, *24*

caves, 20, 30, 39

cedar barrens, 29

cedars, 23

celandine (wood) poppy (*Stylophorum diphyl-
lum*), 24, 49

Center for Wildlife Law, 5

cherrybark oak, 32

chestnut, American (*Castanea dentata*), 9, 22,
23

chestnut oak (*Quercus prinus*), 23, 27

Chinese yam, 9

chinkapin oak (*Quercus muehlenbergii*), 23, 29

Christian County, 28

Christian religion, 14

cinnamon fern (*Osmunda cinnamomea*), 34

Cirriphyllum piliferum, 51

clay soils, 25

clearweed (*Pilea pumila*), 30

cleft phlox (*Phlox bifida*), 161, *162*

clematis, *74*

cliff communities, 29–30, 51, 161–62

climate, changes in, 38–39

climbing bleeding heart, 65

Coastal Plain, 20, *21*, 27. *See also* East Gulf
Coastal Plain; Lower Ohio River Floodplain;
Mississippi River

cobble bars, 34, *34*, 124–25

cocklebur plant, 16

collection of plants, 7, 11-12, 35, 60, 124, 137

collective catastrophe threshold, 41

columbine (*Aquilegia canadensis*), 30

commercial products, biodiversity and, 15–17

common cattail (*Typha latifolia*), 32

common duckweed (*Lemna minor*), 31

common lady fern (*Athyrium filix-femina*),
30

common silverbell (*Halesia tetraptera*), 69

lily-of-the-valley, wild (*Maianthemum canadense*), 50, 67

limestone, 20, 21

    nonforest communities and, 25, 27, 28, 99–100, 101

    seeps and, 137, 139

limestone barrens, 29

limestone fame-flower (*Talinum calcaricum*), *36*, 36–37, *99–100*

limestone flat-rock glade communities, 27

limestone glades, 19, 25, 27, 40

limestone seeps, 137, 139

little bluestem (*Schizachyrium scoparium*), 25, 27, 28, 34, 124

little mountain meadow-rue (*Thalictrum mirabile*), 30

liverworts, 24, 30

lobed spleenwort (*Asplenium pinnatifidum*), 30

loess, 20, 60

logging, 8, 20, 22

Louisville, 5, 99

Lower Ohio River Floodplain, *21, 97, 139, 162*. *See also* Coastal Plain; Interior Low Plateaus

lowland communities, 30

Lucy Braun's white snakeroot (*Ageratina luciae-brauniae*), *164*

lymphoma, 16

magnesium, 99

maidenhair fern (*Adiantum capillus-veneris*), 30

maidenhair spleenwort (*Asplenium trichomanes*), 30

marsh communities, soils of, 32

marshes, *31, 32, 32, 34, 133*

Master, L. L., 3

matricary grape fern (*Botrychium matricarifolium*), *51, 72*

matted feather moss (*Brachythecium populeum*), 51

Maysville, 99

McAlpin Dam, 97

McCreary County, 99

meadow-rue (*Thalictrum mirabile*), 30

meadows, *32, 32, 34*

medicine, biodiversity and, 15

Mercer County, 161

mercury spurge (*Euphorbia mercurialina*), 94

meristem, 98

mesic communities, 19

mesic forests, 23–25

mesic (tall-grass) prairies, 28, *28*

mesophytic characteristcs, 19

Michaux's bluet (*Houstonia serpyllifolia*), 51, *70*

Michaux's saxifrage (*Saxifraga michauxii*), 51, *73*

mid-grass (dry) prairies, 28

military bases, 99

milkwort, *118*

mineral licks, 98

mints, 11

Miscanthus, 9

Mississippi Alluvial Plain, 20, 60

Mississippian Plateau, 25

Mississippi River, 20

mock bishop's weed (*Ptilimnium capillaceum*), *148*

mock-orange (*Philadelphus*), *80, 81*

mosses, 11, 24, 25, 27, 30, 34, 51

mountain fringe, *65*

mountain laurel (*Kalmia latifolia*), 23, *23*

mountain-lover, Canby's (*Paxistima canbyi*), 54, *166*

mountain maple (*Acer spicatum*), 39, *39*, 54

mountain spleenwort (*Asplenium montanum*), 30

mountain sweet pepperbush (*Clethra acuminata*), 24

musk thistle, 9

Muslim religion, 13

Nabhan, G. P., 9

narrowleaf pinweed (*Lechea tenuifolia*), 27

narrow-leaved blue-curls (*Trichostema setaceum*), *114*

narrow-leaved meadowsweet (*Spiraea alba*), *158*

narrow-leaved sunflower, 28

National Association of Home Builders, 7

Native Americans, 20, 28, 60, 135

native giant cane, 24

natural communities, Kentucky, 19–34

Natural Resource and Conservation Service, 7

Natureserve, 3, 13

near-endemics, 36–37

Neckera pennata, 51

necklace glade cress (*Leavenworthia torulosa*), *121*

nettle-leaf sage (*Salvia urticifolia*), *114*

nodding rattlesnake-root (*Prenanthes crepidinea*), *111*

nonforested wetland communities, *32, 32, 34*

northern bog club-moss (*Lycopodium inundatum*), *154*

northern dropseed (*Sporobolus heterolepis*), 98

northern fox grape (*Vitis labrusca*), 15, *15*

northern spicebush (*Lindera benzoin*), 24

northern starflower (*Trientalis borealis*), *53*

northern white cedar (*Thuja occidentalis*), *95*

Nuttall's lobelia (*Lobelia nuttallii*), *136, 137*

oak barrens, 29

oak-hickory forest, 22

oaks, 23, 29

oak wilt, 9

obedient plant (*Physostegia virginiana*), 34, 98, 124

off-road vehicles, 10, 125

Ohio buckeye (*Aesculus glabra*), 24

Ohio River, 21, 97, *139*, 139, 162

O'Keeffe, Georgia, 14

old-growth forests, 20, 22

Oncophorus raui, 51

orange-flowered hoary puccoon (*Lithospermum canescens*), 98

orange-grass (*Hypericum gentianoides*), 27

orchids, *4*, 11, *11*, 35, 37, 40, 42, 70, 76, 98, 99, 126, *135*, 136–37, *152*

Orchid Thief, The (Orleans), 35

Ordovician Age bedrock, 58

Oriental bittersweet, 9

Orleans, Susan, 35

ovate catchfly (*Silene ovata*), 50, 93

ovate false fiddleleaf (*Hydrolea ovata*), *157*

overcollection, 7, 11–12, 35, 60, 124, 137

overcup oak (*Quercus lyrata*), 25, 31

Owen County, 58, 161

painted trillium (*Trillium undulatum*), 50, 51, 54–55, *54*

paleoendemics, 39

pale purple coneflower (*Echinacea simulata*), 27, 28, 97

Palisades, Kentucky River, 56, *57*, 58, 161, *162*

pavement bedrock, 25

pawpaw (*Asimina triloba*), 24

pecan (*Carya illinoinensis*), 31

pellitory (*Parietaria pensylvanica*), 30

penicillin, 16

Pennsylvania pellitory (*Parietaria pensylvanica*), 30

Pennyroyal Plain, 20–21, 27

people, species degradation and, 10–12, 20

peripheral rarity, 39–40

pests, 8–9

pharmaceuticals, 11, 16

Phylloxera vitifoliae, 15

pickerel-weed (*Pontederia cordata*), 157

pignut hickory (*Carya glabra*), 23

Pine Creek barrens, 26

Pine Mountain, *24*, 49, 50–51

pine-oak forest community, 23

pine-oak woodlands, 29

pines, 23

pine woodlands, 29

pinkster-flowered azalea, *33*

pin oak (*Quercus palustris*), 25, 31

pipe-vine (*Aristolochia macrophylla*), 25

pitch pine (*Pinus rigida*), 29

Plant Life of Kentucky (Jones), 42

poison hemlock, 9

poison ivy (*Toxicodendron radicans*), 30

poisonous plants, 9, 30, 55, 100, 137, *138*, 139

poison sumac (*Toxicodendron vernix*), *138*, 139

pollination, 78, 123
    animals and, 54–55, 133, 137
    fragmentation and, 78, 36, 38, 55, 56
    threats to, 9–10

pollinators, threats to, 9–10

pollution, 9–10

Polytrichum pallidisetum, 51

Polytrichum strictum, 51

ponds, 31–32

pondweed, snailseed (*Potamogeton diversifolius*), 31

post oak (*Quercus stellata*), 23

post-oak barrens, 29

poverty dropseed (*Sporobolus vaginiflorus*), 25

Powell County, 99

prairie coneflower (*Ratibida pinnata*), 28, 97

prairie cord grass (*Spartina pectinata*), 28

prairie dock (*Silphium terebinthinaceum*), 28

prairie forbs, 124

prairie gentian (*Gentiana puberulenta*), *108*

prairie June grass, 97, 98–99

prairie rosinweed (*Silphium terebinthinaceum*), 28

prairies, 27–29, *28*, 97–101

Price, Sadie, *109*

Price's aster (*Symphyotrichum priceae*), *109*

Price's potato bean (*Apios priceana*), 44, 60, *60*

prickly-pear cactus (*Opuntia humifusa*), 25

private lands, 4–5

protection, native plant, 3, 11–12, 13–17, 42–44

purple cliffbrake (*Pellaea atropurpurea*), 30

purple-fringed orchid, small (*Platanthera psycodes*), 50, 70

purple prairie-clover (*Dalea purpurea*), 103

purple rattlesnake-root (*Prenanthes racemosa*), 112

Quammen, David, 41

quinine, 16

Rabinowitz, D., 38

racemed milkwort (*Polygala polygama*), 118

ragweed (*Ambrosia artemisiifolia*), 34

Rand's goldenrod (*Solidago randii*), *131*

Rare Plant Recognition Act, 5, 42, 45

rarity, 35–40
    factors influencing, 38
    peripheral, 39–40

ravines, 23, 36, 51

recreational activities, 10, 14

red buckeye (*Aesculus pavia*), 73

redbud, eastern (*Cercis canadensis*), 25, 27

red elderberry (*Sambucus racemosa* ssp. *pubens*), 50, 63

red maple (*Acer rubrum*), 23, 31

red oak, 24

Red River, 10, 123

red-twig doghobble (*Leucothoe recurva*), 51

regulations, native plant, 5

relicts, 38–39

relocation, rare plant, 11, 44

rhododendrons, 24, *159*

ringseed rush (*Juncus filipendulus*), 99

river birch (*Betula nigra*), 31

river communities

    cobble bars and, 34, *34*, 124–25

    dam construction and, 8, 97, 139

    floods and, 31, 123–24, 125

    soil and, 34, 124–25

Roan Mountain goldenrod (*Solidago roanensis*), 50, *66*

Roan Mountain sedge (*Carex roanensis*), 50

rockcastle aster (*Eurybia saxicastellii*), 125, *125*

Rockcastle River, 123

rock climbing, 10

rock harlequin (*Corydalis sempervirens*), 51, *117*

rockhouses, 30, 36, 161–62

rock polypody (*Polypodium virginianum*), 30

rock skullcap (*Scutellaria saxatilis*), 96

root systems, 97, 123, 125, 137

rose-mallow (*Hibiscus moscheutos*), 32

rose pogonia (*Pogonia ophioglossoides*), 4, 51

rose turtlehead (*Chelone obliqua* var. *speciosa*), *155*

rosy periwinkle, 16

rosy twisted stalk (*Streptopus lanceolatus*), 50, *61*

rounded catchfly, 30

round-fruited Saint-John's-wort, 27

round-headed bush-clover (*Lespedeza capitata*), *146*

roundleaf fame-flower, 100, *100*

royal catchfly (*Silene regia*), 8, *8*, 28, 99

royal fern (*Osmunda regalis*), 34

running buffalo clover (*Trifolium stoloniferum*), 44, 58–60, *58*

rushes, 32, 98

rushfoil (*Crotonopsis elliptica*), 25, 27

rust fungus, *127*

Saint-John's-wort (*Hypericum*), 27, *147*

Saint-Peter's-wort (*Hypericum crux-andreae*), *147*

sand grape (*Vitis rupestris*), *130*

sandstone, 20, 25, 27, 28

sandstone barrens, 29

sandstone glades, 25, 27

sandworts, 27, *162*

scarlet Indian paintbrush (*Castilleja coccinea*), 101, *101*

scarlet oak (*Quercus coccinea*), 23

sedges, 32, 54, 89, 98, *115*, 154

sedum, 30

seed dispersal

    animals and, 54–55, 133, 137

    fragmentation and, 7–8, 36, 38, 55, 56

    threats to, 9–10

seeps, 32, *33*, 34, 37–38, 135–37, 139

seminatural communities, 34

shagbark hickory (*Carya ovata*), 23, 24

shaggy hedge hyssop (*Gratiola pilosa*), *144*

shale, 19, 20, 21, 25, 27

Shawnee Hills, 20, *21*, 25, 29, 31. *See also* Interior Low Plateaus

shining ladies'-tresses (*Spiranthes lucida*), *126*

shooting star (*Dodecatheon meadia*), 30

Short, C. W., 97

shortbristle beak-rush (*Rhynchospora corniculata*), 32

shortleaf pine (*Pinus echinata*), 29

Short's goldenrod (*Solidago shortii*), 37, *37*, 44, 97–98

Short's hedge hyssop (*Gratiola viscidula*), *144*

showy gentian (*Gentiana decora*), 19, 51, 68

showy lady's-slipper (*Cypripedium reginae*), 41, *42*

shrubs, 24, 25, 31

shrub swamps, 32

Shumard's oak (*Quercus shumardii*), 24

side-oats grama (*Bouteloua curtipendula*), *108*

silphium sunflower (*Helianthus silphioides*), *149*

silverling (*Paronychia argyrocoma*), 161, *161*

silver maple (*Acer saccharinum*), 31

sinkholes, 20, 31

slender blazing-star (*Liatris cylindracea*), *103*

slender marsh pink (*Sabatia campanulata*), *151*

slopes, 23, 25

sloughs, 30–31

small enchanter's nightshade (*Ciracea alpina*), 51, 53, *53*

small-flower baby-blue-eyes (*Nemophila aphylla*), 59, 60

small purple-fringed orchid (*Platanthera psycodes*), 50, 70

small skullcap (*Scutellaria parvula*), 27

smallspike false nettle (*Boehmeria cylindrica*), 31

small sundrops (*Oenothera perennis*), 51, *105*

small white lady's-slipper (*Cypripedium candidum*), 40, *40*

small yellow lady's-slipper (*Cypripedium parviflorum*), 76

smartweed (*Polygonum*), 32, 34

smooth blackberry (*Rubus canadensis*), 50, *53*, 53–54

smooth cliffbrake (*Pellaea glabella*), 30

smooth phlox (*Phlox glaberrima*), 34

snailseed pondweed (*Potamogeton diversifolius*), 31

snow squarestem (*Melanthera nivea*), 75

snow trillium (*Trillium nivale*), 85

soft-haired thermopsis (*Thermopsis mollis*), 4

soft-hairy false gromwell (*Onosmodium molle*), 113

softleaf arrowwood (*Viburnum molle*), 92

soil

  ATVs and, 125

  forests and, 23, 25

  glade communities and, 25, 27, 99–100, 101

  prairie communities and, 28, 99

  river communities and, 124–25

  water movement through, 25

  wetland communities and, 31–32

  See also bedrock; limestone; loess; sandstone; shale

Song of the Dodo: Island Biogeography in an Age of Extinction (Quammen), 41

sourwood (*Oxydendrum arboreum*), 23

southern crabapple, 42

southern heartleaf (*Hexastylis contracta*), 51, 55, 55

southern mountain cranberry (*Vaccinium erythrocarpu*), 50

southern red oak (*Quercus falcata*), 23

southern wild rice, 32, 135

special concern, plants of, 41, 42

sphagnum moss (*Sphagnum quinquefarium*), 34, 51

spiked blazing-star (*Liatris spicata*), 19

spiked hoary pea (*Tephrosia spicata*), 126

spines, 97

spinulose wood fern (*Dryopteris ludoviciana*), 50

spleenwort, 30

spoon-leaved sundew (*Drosera intermedia*), 140

spotted coral-root (*Corallorhiza maculata*), 86

spotted joe-pye weed (*Eupatorium maculatum*), 50

spotted mandarin (*Prosartes maculata*), 76

spotted wintergreen (*Chimaphila maculata*), 23

spray cliffs, 51

spring beauty (*Claytonia*), 49

springs, 32

star tickseed (*Coreopsis pubescens*), 89

Steele's joe-pye weed (*Eupatorium steelei*), 50, 51, 64

stemless evening primrose (*Oenothera triloba*), 116

stipuled scurfpea, 3, 41

stitchwort, water (*Sagina fontinalis*), 30

streams, 20, 31, 38, 123–25

submerged aquatics, 123, 133

subterranean streams, 21

subxeric (dry) forests, 23

succulents, 97, 100, 162

sugar maple (*Acer saccharum*), 24, 25

summer sedge, 50

sunflowers, 28, 98, 99

Svenson's wild rye (*Elymus svensonii*), 161

swamp candle (*Lysimachia terrestris*), 147

swamp cottonwood (*Populus heterophylla*), 31

swamp rose (*Rosa palustris*), 31

swamps, 30–31, 31, 31–32, 133

swamp tupelo (*Nyssa aquatica*), 30

sweet birch, 24

sweet coneflower (*Rudbeckia subtomentosa*), 28, 107

sweet fern (*Comptonia peregrina*), 131

sweetgum (*Liquidambar styraciflua*), 31, 32

sweet pepperbush (*Clethra acuminata*), 24

sweet pinesap (*Monotropsis odorata*), 78

sweetscent ladies'-tresses (*Spiranthes odorata*), 152

sweetshrub (*Calycanthus floridus*), 55, 129

sweet white violet (*Viola blanda*), 30

Swenson's wild rye, 162

switchgrass (*Panicum virgatum*), 28

swollen bladderwort (*Utricularia inflata*), 43

tall-grass (mesic) prairies, 28

tall hairy groovebur (*Agrimonia gryposepala*), 50

tall tickseed (*Coreopsis tripteris*), 28

tansy rosinweed (*Silphium pinnatifidum*), 113

taproots, 97

tawny cotton-grass (*Eriophorum virginicum*), 153

Taxol, 16

ten-lobe false foxglove (*Agalinis obtusifolia*), 56, 121

Tennessee aster (*Eurybia hemispherica*), 143

Tennessee bladder fern (*Cystopteris tennesseensis*), 30

Tennessee leafcup (*Polymnia laevigata*), 59, 60

teosinte, 15–16

thread-foot (*Podostemum ceratophyllum*), 10, 123–24

threatened species designation, 41

three-awn grass, 25, 28

tourism, 14

trade, international, 11

trailing arbutus (*Epigaea repens*), 23

trails, animal, 58–60, 97

transplantation, 11, 44

tree-of-heaven, 9

trepocarpus (*Trepocarpus aethusae*), 129

trillium, 11, 24, 49, 49, 54, 54–55, 84, 85

tropical rain forests, 16

trumpet creeper (*Campsis radicans*), 30